Journal of The Institute of Reformed Baptist Studies

A theological journal committed to confessional Reformed Baptist theology

The Journal of the Institute of Reformed Baptist Studies (*JIRBS*)

Purchasing instructions

JIRBS is published on an annual basis. Individual issues can be purchased for $12 USD (plus shipping and handling). If paying by check, make it payable to **RBAP** and write the issue(s) purchasing on the memo line (e.g., *JIRBS* 2014). Email rb@rbap.net for orders being paid via check so shipping and handling can be calculated. All back issues are available. Send your check made out to **RBAP** to the following address:

RBAP
c/o Richard Barcellos
349 Sunrise Terrace
Palmdale, CA 93551

On the memo line, please include the issue(s) purchasing.

JIRBS may be purchased electronically at www.rbap.net.

Correspondence

General correspondence can be sent to the address above. Email correspondence should be directed to rb@rbap.net.

Published by RBAP, Palmdale, CA
www.rbap.net
Printed in the United States of America.

Cover and formatted for print by Cameron Porter.

ISBN-13: 978-1507771846
ISBN-10: 1507771843

SCOPUS SCRIPTURAE:

John Owen, Nehemiah Coxe, our Lord Jesus Christ, and a Few Early Disciples on Christ as the Scope of Scripture

Richard C. Barcellos*

Terms such as Christ-centered and Christocentric are used often in our day. But what do they mean? The older way of describing the concept these terms point to, the target or end to which all of the Bible tends, is encapsulated by the Latin phrase *scopus Scripturae* (i.e., the scope of the Scriptures). This concept gained confessional status in the Westminster Confession of Faith, the Savoy Declaration, and the Second London Baptist Confession of Faith in 1.5, which, speaking of Holy Scripture, says, ". . . the scope of the whole (which is to give all glory to God)..." Reformation and post-Reformation Reformed theologians understood scope in two senses. It had a narrow sense—i.e., the scope of a given text or passage, its basic thrust. But it also had a wider sense—i.e., the target or bull's eye to which all of Scripture tends.[1] It is with this second sense that we will give our attention. The goal of this study is to identify the Reformed concept of Christ as *scopus Scripturae* and to attempt to show that it is firmly grounded in Holy Scripture itself.

We will give some space to the historical-theological background to the issue and then use John Owen and Nehemiah Coxe as examples of two within the Reformed orthodox theological tradition who articulated Christ as the scope of Scripture. Once the

---

* Richard C. Barcellos, Ph.D., is pastor of Grace Reformed Baptist Church, Palmdale, CA (www.grbcav.org). He is author of *The Lord's Supper as a Means of Grace: More than a Memory* and *Better than the Beginning: Creation in Biblical Perspective*. English Bible references are from the New American Standard Bible Updated Edition.

[1] See the discussion in Richard A. Muller, *Post-Reformation Reformed Dogmatics: The Rise and Development of Reformed Orthodoxy, ca. 1520 to ca. 1725, Volume Two – Holy Scripture* (Grand Rapids: Baker Academic, 2003 [Second Edition]), 206-23, where he discusses these distinctions.

historical section is completed, a brief attempt will be made to illustrate the same concept assumed in and being applied by the words of our Lord Jesus Christ and some of his early disciples. The article will conclude with a challenge to utilize this hermeneutical principle in our interpretations of Holy Scripture.

Some Historical-Theological Background on *Scopus Scripturae*

The post-Reformation Reformed orthodox theologians embraced a whole-Bible hermeneutic. This manifested itself in their understanding of the scope of Scripture.[2] Though *scopus* could refer to the immediate pericope, it also had a wider, redemptive-historical focus. *Scopus*, in this latter sense, referred to the center or target of the entirety of canonical revelation or that to which the entire Bible points. For the seventeenth-century Reformed orthodox and their Reformed predecessors, Christ was the scope of Scripture, being the primary means through which God gets glory for himself.

The *First Helvetic Confession* of 1536 gave early Reformed expression to this concept in Article V, entitled the Scope of Scripture.[3] The first sentence of that article reads as follows:

> The position of this entire canonical scripture [or of the entire actual canonical scripture] is this, that God is kindhearted [or shows kindness] to the race of men, and that he has proclaimed [or demonstrated] this kindness [or goodwill] through Christ his Son.[4]

The title of Article V indicates that the concept of the scope of Scripture goes back to at least 1536 (among the Reformed) and that

---

[2] For a helpful historically and theologically aware introduction to this concept see Muller, *PRRD*, II:206-23. Cf. also Martin I. Klauber, "Hermeneutics and the Doctrine of Scripture in Post-Reformation Reformed Thought," *Premise*, Volume II, Number 9 (October 19, 1995): 8ff. and James M. Renihan, "Theology on Target: The Scope of the Whole," *Reformed Baptist Theological Review*, II:2 (July 2005): 36-53.

[3] Cf. Philip Schaff, *The Creeds of Christendom, Volume III: The Evangelical Protestant Creeds* (Grand Rapids: Baker Books, Reprinted 1996), 212.

[4] This English translation of the original Latin was provided by Amy Chifici, M.A. Cf. Schaff, *Creeds, III*, 212-13, for the German and Latin originals.

Christ was seen as the revelation of God's kindness to man. This is the position of the "entire canonical scripture."

In 1629, William Ames said, "The Old and New Testaments are reducible to these two primary heads. The Old promises Christ to come and the New testifies that he has come."[5] The concept of Christ as the scope of Scripture is clear in Ames.

Isaac Ambrose gives eloquent expression to the concept of Christ as the scope of Scripture in later Reformed thought:

> Keep still Jesus Christ in your eye, in the perusal of the Scriptures, as the end, scope and substance thereof: what are the whole Scriptures, but as it were the spiritual swaddling clothes of the holy child Jesus? 1. Christ is the truth and substance of all the types and shadows. 2. Christ is the substance and matter of the Covenant of Grace, and all administrations thereof; under the Old Testament Christ is veiled, under the New Covenant revealed. 3. Christ is the centre and meeting place of all the promises; for in him the promises of God are yea and Amen. 4. Christ is the thing signified, sealed and exhibited in the Sacraments of the Old and New Testament. 5. Scripture genealogies use to lead us on to the true line of Christ. 6. Scripture chronologies are to discover to us the times and seasons of Christ. 7. Scripture-laws are our schoolmasters to bring us to Christ, the moral by correcting, the ceremonial by directing. 8. Scripture-gospel is Christ's light, whereby we hear and follow him; Christ's cords of love, whereby we are drawn into sweet union and communion with him; yea it is the very power of God unto salvation unto all them that believe in Christ Jesus; and therefore think of Christ as the very substance, marrow, soul and scope of the whole Scriptures.[6]

Richard A. Muller, commenting on *scopus* in seventeenth-century Reformed thought, says:

---

[5] William Ames, *The Marrow of Theology* (Durham, NC: The Labyrinth Press, 1983), 202 (XXXVIII:5).

[6] Isaac Ambrose, *Works* (1701), 201, as quoted in J. I. Packer, *A Quest for Godliness: The Puritan Vision of the Christian Life* (Wheaton, IL: Crossway Books, 1990), 103.

> Christ . . . is the *fundamentum* and *scopus* of Scripture inasmuch as he is the redemptive center on which the entire *principium cognoscendi* or cognitive foundation rests and in whom it find [*sic*] its unity.[7]

> . . . the theologies of the Reformers and of their orthodox successors consistently place Christ at the center of their discussions of redemption, consistently understand Christ as the center and fulfillment of divine revelation, and equally consistently understand the causality of salvation as grounded in the divine purpose. Christ, as Mediator, must be subordinate to the divine purpose, even as Christ, considered as God, is the one who with the Father and the Spirit decrees salvation before the foundation of the world: Causal theocentricity guarantees redemptive Christocentricity. Neither the doctrine of God nor the doctrine of Christ, however, serves as the basis of a neatly deduced system: The *loci* themselves arise out of the interpretation of Scripture.[8]

According to seventeenth-century Reformed orthodoxy, then, Christ is the target to which the whole of Scripture tends. This view of the scope of Scripture was closely related to their view of the relation between the testaments, seen in terms of a promise/fulfillment, figure/reality, type/anti-type motif.[9] Hence, "the New Testament may be understood as the interpreter of the Old."[10] Revelation was progressive, self-interpreting, and consummated in the coming of Christ.

Here we must be careful not to infuse later, neo-orthodox concepts of Christocentricity into the historical data. The Christocentricity of the Reformed and Reformed orthodox was redemptive-historical and revelational, not principial, as Muller points out.[11] In other words, it came as a result of Scripture

---

7 Richard A. Muller, "Calvin and the "Calvinists": Assessing Continuities and Discontinuities Between the Reformation and Orthodoxy," *Calvin Theological Journal* 30 (1995): 156.

8 Muller, "Calvin and the "Calvinists"," 155.

9 Muller, *PRRD*, II:492.

10 Muller, *PRRD*, II:492.

11 Muller, "Calvin and the "Calvinists"," 157.

functioning as the *principium cognoscendi* (i.e., principle of knowing) or cognitive foundation of our knowledge of God. Scripture, and not Christ the Mediator, is a fundamental principle or foundation of theology in Reformed orthodoxy.[12] They started with Scripture and concluded Christocentricity in terms of the *historia salutis*. Their Christocentricity is revelational and connected to redemption. As Muller says, such "Christocentrism consistently places Christ at the historical and at the soteriological center of the work of redemption."[13] But we must still be careful with the term Christocentricity. Christology must not be viewed as the central dogma of the Reformed orthodox. As Muller says:

> Such doctrines as God, predestination, Christ, and covenant provide not alternative but coordinate *foci*—and the presence of each and every one of these topics in theology rests not on a rational, deductive process but on their presence as *loci* in the exegetical or interpretive tradition of the church.[14]

The method of Reformed orthodoxy, then, started with the text of Scripture and its exegesis. Christ as the scope of Scripture was a conclusion from Scripture not a presupposition brought to Scripture. The Reformed orthodox Christocentric interpretation of the Bible was an attempt at applying a principle derived from the Bible and an application of *sola Scriptura* to the issue of hermeneutics. In other words, they recognized the authority of Scripture in the interpretation of Scripture. Christ as the scope of Scripture conditioned all subsequent interpretation, to varying degrees depending upon the interpreter.

John Owen on Christ as *Scopus Scripturae*

Christ as the scope of Scripture can be seen in Owen's writings in many places. In his work on the person of Christ, Owen says, "The

---

[12] Richard A. Muller, *Dictionary of Latin and Greek Theological Terms* (Grand Rapids: Baker Book House, 1985, Second printing, September 1986), 245-46.

[13] Muller, "Calvin and the "Calvinists"," 157.

[14] Muller, "Calvin and the "Calvinists"," 157.

end of the Word itself, is to instruct us in the knowledge of God in Christ."[15] A few pages later he goes on to say:

> Christ is the image of the invisible God, the express image of the person of the Father; and *the principal end* of the whole Scripture, especially of the Gospel, is to declare him so to be, and how he is so.[16]

In these two instances Owen uses the term 'end' in a technical sense. In other words, Christ is the scope of Scripture.

Christ as *scopus Scripturae* can be seen from an exegetical standpoint in Owen as well. Commenting on Genesis 3:15 as the first promise of the only means of delivery from the effects of sin–Christ, Owen says:

> This is the very foundation of the faith of the church; and if it be denied, nothing of the economy or dispensation of God towards it from the beginning can be understood. The whole doctrine and story of the Old Testament must be rejected as useless, and no foundation be left in the truth of God for the introduction of the New.[17]

Without a soteriological/Messianic interpretation of Genesis 3:15, in the mind of Owen, subsequent Scripture makes no sense. A Christocentric hermeneutic is foundational for proper biblical interpretation.

In his "Exercitations on the Epistle to the Hebrews," Owen says:

> The great design, whose lines are drawn in the face, and whose substance lies in the bowels of the Old Testament, and which is the spirit that enlivens the whole doctrine and story of it, the bond of union wherein all the parts do centre, without which they would be loose, scattered, and deformed heaps, is the bringing

---

[15] John Owen, *The Works of John Owen*, 23 vols., ed. William H. Goold (Edinburgh: The Banner of Truth Trust, 1987 edition), 1:65. Emphasis added.

[16] Owen, *Works*, 1:74. Emphasis added.

[17] Owen, *Works*, 1:120. Cf. Richard Daniels, *The Christology of John Owen* (Grand Rapids: Reformation Heritage Books, 2004), 230-61.

> forth of the Messiah, the Saviour of the world. Without an apprehension of this design, and faith therein, neither can a letter of it be understood, nor can a rational man discover any important excellency in it. *Him* it promiseth, *him* it typifieth, *him* it teacheth and prophesieth about, *him* it calls all men to desire and expect.[18]

Owen, writing on the "Oneness of the Church" throughout redemptive history, argues that the object of saving faith throughout that history is "the *Seed* that was in the promise . . ."[19] In this brief exercitation, Owen argues that God first gave the promise of salvation to Adam based on Genesis 3:15. In fact, God's Church is founded "in the promise of the Messiah given to Adam."[20] Owen argues that all subsequent revelation serves to unfold the first promise of the gospel to Adam. This promise is the first revelation of the covenant of grace.[21] Subsequent revelation unfolds the promise of the Redeemer and, in fact, depends upon it.

Returning to Owen's treatise on the person of Christ, he says:

> This principle is always to be retained in our minds in reading of the Scripture,—namely, that the revelation and doctrine of the person of Christ and his office, is the foundation whereon all other instructions of the prophets and apostles for the edification of the church are built, and whereinto they are resolved; as is declared, Eph. ii. 20-22. So our Lord Jesus Christ himself at large makes it manifest, Luke xxiv. 26, 27, 45, 46. Lay aside the consideration hereof, and the Scriptures are no such thing as they pretend unto,—namely, a revelation of the glory of God in the salvation of the church; nor are those of the Old Testament so at this day unto the Jews, who own not this principle, 2 Cor. iii. 13-16. There are, therefore, such revelations of the person and glory of Christ treasured up in the Scripture, from the beginning unto the end of it, as may exercise the faith and contemplation of believers in this world, and shall never, during this life, be fully discovered or

---

18 Owen, *Works*, 17:370.
19 Owen, *Works*, 17:121, 142.
20 Owen, *Works*, 17:120.
21 Owen, *Works*, 17:120.

> understood; and in divine meditations of these revelations doth much of the life of faith consist.[22]

For Owen, "the revelation and doctrine of the person of Christ and his office" is the hermeneutical key providing interpretive cohesiveness for all of Scripture.

Owen's Christocentricity has been identified by several recent studies. In an article on John Owen dealing with his *Dissertation on Divine Justice* and subtitled "An Exercise in Christocentric Scholasticism," Carl Trueman says, ". . . his theology is, at heart, thoroughly christocentric."[23] Trueman entitles his conclusion "Owen's Christocentrism" and says:

> In asserting the necessity of Christ's sacrifice, Owen is presenting a Reformed theology that cannot displace the historical person of the mediator from the center of the drama of redemption. There can be no eternal justification based purely on the decree: Salvation is as surely linked to history as it is to eternity. It is those who predicate the necessity of incarnation and atonement solely on the decretive will of God who run the risk of marginalizing the historical person of Christ and undermining the importance of salvation history. In this context, Owen's scholasticism serves not to eclipse Christ but to place him at the center. Indeed, as is clear from his argument, if it was not for his Thomist understanding of God's causal relationship to creation and his acceptance of the validity of the analogy of being, Owen would have no way of attacking his opponents' position. While it is true that his use of such arguments depends on assumptions that he does not justify, it is also true that any rejection of their validity renders his christocentrism epistemologically unsustainable. In the context of this dispute, at least, it is the rejection of natural theology, not its acceptance, that is the enemy of Christ-centered theology.[24]

---

22 Owen, *Works*, 1:314-15.

23 Carl R. Trueman, "John Owen's *Dissertation on Divine Justice*: An Exercise in Christocentric Scholasticism," *Calvin Theological Journal* 33 (1998): 97.

24 Trueman, "John Owen's *Dissertation on Divine Justice*," 103.

In fact, Trueman goes so far as to say that on the issue of divine justice and the incarnation, Owen "is arguably not less christocentric than [his] opponents, including Calvin himself, but actually more so."[25]

Kelly M. Kapic says of John Owen:

> For Owen, all Scripture points to Christ, for "the revelation of the person of Christ and his office, is the foundation whereon all other instructions of the prophets and apostles for the edification of the church are built and whereinto they are resolved" (Works, 1:314-15). Owen attempts to avoid allowing the original context and meaning of any Old Testament passage to be lost; yet, he also maintains that a Christian exegete must ultimately find the passage's Christological meaning.[26]

He argues that Owen's anthropology is formulated "in a christocentric pattern, pointing to Jesus Christ as the incarnate and true image of God."[27] Even the Sabbath is Christologically transformed by Christ, thus further displaying the Christocentricity of Owen's thought.[28]

Sebastian Rehnman says of Owen, "His theology has, for all its adherence to scholasticism and contrary to the argument of much modern scholarship on Reformed orthodoxy, a Christocentric and practical character."[29]

Richard W. Daniels shows that not only redemption, but creation and providence are Christocentric for Owen.[30] Commenting on the doctrines of creation and providence in Owen's thought, Daniels says, "It is difficult to conceive of a more

---

[25] Trueman, "John Owen's *Dissertation on Divine Justice*," 103.

[26] Kelly M. Kapic, "Owen, John (*1616-1683*)" in Donald K. McKim, editor, *Dictionary of Major Biblical Interpreters*, 797-98.

[27]Kelly M. Kapic, *Communion with God: The Divine and the Human in the Theology of John Owen* (Grand Rapids: Baker Academic, 2007), 65.

[28] Kapic, *Communion with God*, 212-14. Cf. Owen, *Works*, 18:263-460 for Owen's masterful treatment of a day of sacred rest.

[29] Sebastian Rehnman, *Divine Discourse: The Theological Methodology of John Owen* (Grand Rapids: Baker Academic, 2002), 181.

[30] Daniels, *Christology of Owen*, 178-93.

Christocentric view of the purpose of God in creation than this, which subjects the creation and history of the universe to the manifestation of the glory of God in its renovation by the Son."[31] After acknowledging that Owen's Christocentricity was not unique among the English Puritans, he then says:

> In the development of this Christocentric theological system, however, Owen was unsurpassed. The lines which he traces from the doctrine of the person of Christ are bold, and long enough to reach every subject of doctrinal inquiry, showing that "by him, all things" [including all doctrinal truths] consist" (Col. 1:17).[32]

In Daniels' concluding words to his study on Owen's Christology, he gives this tribute to him:

> [I]t is one thing to say Christian theology ought to be Christocentric, it is quite another to actually understand the entire spectrum of theological *loci* Christocentrically, or to articulate one's theology in a way that manifests this Christocentricity. Owen does this, as we have observed with regard to the knowledge of God, creation, providence, the redemption of man, the mediatorial kingdom, the church, and the Christian life.[33]

According to John Owen, Christ is the scope of Scripture.

Nehemiah Coxe on Christ as *Scopus Scripturae*

Nehemiah Coxe was a Particular Baptist.[34] He is important in our brief survey for at least two reasons: 1) Coxe was the co-editor (and

---

31 Daniels, *Christology of Owen*, 180.

32 Daniels, *Christology of Owen*, 517. Bracketed words are Daniels'.

33 Daniels, *Christology of Owen*, 519.

34 For a brief biography cf. James M. Renihan, "An Excellent and Judicious Divine: Nehemiah Coxe" in Nehemiah Coxe and John Owen, edited by Ronald D. Miller, James M. Renihan, and Francisco Orozco, *Covenant Theology From Adam to Christ* (Owensboro, KY: Reformed Baptist Academic Press, 2005), 7-24; James M. Renihan, "Confessing the Faith in 1644 and 1689" in *Reformed Baptist Theological Review*, III:1 (July 2006): 33ff.; and Michael A. G. Haykin, *Kiffin, Knollys and Keach*

most likely the "senior" editor) of the Particular Baptist *Second London Confession of Faith* (2LCF)[35] and 2) he authored *A Discourse of the Covenants that God made with men before the Law . . .*, which is structured after the federal model, utilizes Reformed orthodox theological nomenclature, concepts, and sources, and is semantically Reformed orthodox, except portions of his exposition of the Abrahamic covenant(s).[36]

In his Discourse of the Covenants, he says:

> 11. It was from this design of love and mercy that when the Lord God came to fallen man in the garden in the cool of the day, and found him filled with horror and shame in the consciousness of his own guilt, he did not execute the rigor of the law on him. Instead he held a treaty with him which issued in a discovery of grace. By this a door of hope was opened to him in the laying of a new foundation for his acceptance with God and walking well pleasing before him.
> 1. For in the sentence passed on the serpent (which principally involved the Devil whose instrument he had been in tempting man, and who probably was made to abide in his possession of the serpent until he had received this doom, Genesis 3:15) there was couched a blessed promise of redemption and salvation to man. This was to be worked out by the Son of God made of a woman, and so her seed, and man was to receive the promised salvation by faith and to hope in it. In this implied promise was laid the first foundation of the church after the fall of man which was to be raised up out of the ruins of the Devil's kingdom by the destruction of his work by Jesus Christ (1 John 3:8).[37]

Coxe adds later:

> From the first dawning of the blessed light of God's grace to poor sinners faintly displayed in the promise intimated in Genesis 3:15,

---

(Leeds, England: Reformation Today Trust, 1996) for an introduction to three key Particular Baptists of the seventeenth century.

[35] Cf. Renihan, "An Excellent and Judicious Divine: Nehemiah Coxe," 19-21 and Renihan, "Confessing the Faith in 1644 and 1689," 33ff.

[36] Cf. Coxe and Owen, *Covenant Theology*, 71-140.

[37] Coxe and Owen, *Covenant Theology*, 55.

> the redeemed of the Lord were brought into a new relation to God, in and by Christ the promised seed, through faith in him as revealed in that promise.[38]

This understanding of Genesis 3:15 gives Coxe's work a Christocentric flavor from the beginning. In the first paragraph of his work, he says:

> The great interest of man's present peace and eternal happiness is most closely concerned in religion. And all true religion since the fall of man must be taught by divine revelation which God by diverse parts and after a diverse manner[39] has given out to his church. He caused this light gradually to increase until the whole mystery of his grace was perfectly revealed in and by Jesus Christ in whom are hid all the treasures of wisdom and knowledge. God, whose works were all known by him from the beginning, has in all ages disposed and ordered the revelation of his will to men, his transactions with them, and all the works of his holy providence toward them, with reference to the fullness of time and the gathering of all things to a head in Christ Jesus. So in all our search after the mind of God in the Holy Scriptures we are to manage our inquiries with reference to Christ. Therefore the best interpreter of the Old Testament is the Holy Spirit speaking to us in the new. There we have the clearest light of the knowledge of the glory of God shining on us in the face of Jesus Christ, by unveiling those counsels of love and grace that were hidden from former ages and generations.[40]

Not only is this statement programmatic for a Christocentric understanding of Scripture, it also reflects the fact that Coxe viewed special revelation as progressive. The 2LCF, 7:2 says, "This covenant is revealed in the Gospel; first of all to Adam in the promise of Salvation by the seed of the woman, and afterwards by farther steps, until the full discovery thereof was completed in the

---

38 Coxe and Owen, *Covenant Theology*, 59.

39 Here he is dependent upon Beza. Cf. Coxe and Owen, *Covenant Theology*, 33, n.1.

40 Coxe and Owen, *Covenant Theology*, 33.

new Testament." Coxe saw Christ as the hermeneutical center and focal-point of the whole Bible (i.e., its *scopus*). Coxe understood redemptive revelation as progressive and Christo-telic.

Christ, according to Nehemiah Coxe, is the scope of Scripture.

Our Lord Jesus on Christ as *Scopus Scripturae*

Commenting on the New Testament's view of the Old Testament as a witness to Christ, Richard Gaffin says:

> For Jesus and the New Testament writers the Old Testament is one large prophetic and promissory witness to Christ, a diverse but unified witness that centers in his sufferings and consequent glorification. The Old Testament has its overall integrity, its various parts cohere, in terms of this death-and-resurrection focus.
>
> Put negatively, the Old Testament does not have multiple and discordant trajectories of meaning, but only one. That is the unidirectional path that leads to Christ, however obscure and difficult it may be for us to follow that path at points along the way.[41]

Probably the most often cited words of our Lord to illustrate his view of himself in terms of Scripture occur at the end of Luke's Gospel (Luke 24:25-27 and 44-47). But John's Gospel contains a severe rebuke by Jesus of some Jewish leaders which may illustrate Gaffin's point above even better than Luke 24. Listen to these words by Jesus:

> Do not think that I will accuse you before the Father; the one who accuses you is Moses, in whom you have set your hope. For if you believed Moses, you would believe Me, for he wrote about Me. But if you do not believe his writings, how will you believe My words? (John 5:45-47)

---

[41] Richard B. Gaffin Jr., ""For Our Sakes Also": Christ in the Old Testament in the New Testament" in Robert L. Penny ed., *The Hope Fulfilled: Essays in Honor of O. Palmer Robertson* (Phillipsburg, NJ: P&R Publishing, 2008), 79.

These words were spoken after Jesus had said, "You search the Scriptures because you think that in them you have eternal life; it is these that testify about Me" (John 5:39). The more inclusive statement (5:39) is followed by a specific statement concentrating on the writings of Moses (5:45-47). These texts indicate not only that Jesus viewed the Old Testament as a witness to himself but that it functioned this way apart from his own self-witness. In other words, the Old Testament was a Messianic document on its own. Commenting on these texts, Gaffin says:

> Here Jesus affirms the relative overall clarity and independence of Moses (the Old Testament), as a witness to himself, distinct from his own teaching (and so, by implication, of the New Testament). So much is the case that this Old Testament witness to Christ serves as an adequate basis for the just condemnation of those rejecting him (verse 45), in itself and independent of his own self-witness.[42]

These words of Jesus illustrate that he viewed the Old Testament as a perspicuous witness to himself. Read in conjunction with Luke 24:25-27 and 44-47, it seems clear that Jesus viewed the Old Testament as a whole finding its goal in him.

I will assume that my readers agree that Jesus viewed himself as the scope of Scripture and follow this brief discussion about our Lord with a look at some of his early disciples.

Some Early Disciples on Christ as *Scopus Scripturae*

The discussion in this section is very limited in scope. I will not attempt to look at the New Testament use of the Old Testament as proof of Christ as *scopus Scripturae*, though I think that could be done with much profit and support my thesis. Instead, I want to look briefly at John 2. In this passage, we will note that some early disciples give evidence of the concept of Christ as the scope of Scripture. Here is John 2:13-22.

---

[42] Gaffin, ""For Our Sakes Also,"" 75.

> The Passover of the Jews was near, and Jesus went up to Jerusalem. And He found in the temple those who were selling oxen and sheep and doves, and the money changers seated *at their tables*. And He made a scourge of cords, and drove *them* all out of the temple, with the sheep and the oxen; and He poured out the coins of the money changers and overturned their tables; and to those who were selling the doves He said, "Take these things away; stop making My Father's house a place of business." His disciples remembered that it was written, "ZEAL FOR YOUR HOUSE WILL CONSUME ME." The Jews then said to Him, "What sign do You show us as your authority for doing these things?" Jesus answered them, "Destroy this temple, and in three days I will raise it up." The Jews then said, "It took forty-six years to build this temple, and will You raise it up in three days?" But He was speaking of the temple of His body. So when He was raised from the dead, His disciples remembered that He said this; and they believed the Scripture and the word which Jesus had spoken.

We often think of hermeneutics, interpreting the Bible, as something we do. That is true. However, notice verses 17 and 22 of John 2. John 2:17 begins by saying, "His disciples remembered that it was written . . ." This is John's commentary on the thought process of some of Christ's disciples in the first century prior to the writing of the New Testament. The words "it was written" refer to what was already written at that time. John tells us what "was written" and what Old Testament text these disciples were thinking about by quoting Psalm 69:9, "ZEAL FOR YOUR HOUSE WILL CONSUME ME" (Cf. John 15:25 and 19:28 where Jesus applies this Psalm to himself.). The disciples were interpreting the Old Testament (independent of the New Testament) during the life of our Lord. John's comment informs us that they started connecting the dots from the Psalms to Jesus while our Lord was on the earth. In other words, their minds were making hermeneutical moves while Christ's zeal for God's temple, his Father's house, was being manifested. As the Word who became flesh manifested himself among men, those who believed in him began to interpret Scripture in light of him (or him in light of Scripture!).

John 2:22 says, "So when He was raised from the dead, His disciples remembered that He said this; and they believed the Scripture and the word which Jesus had spoken." Note first the time when "His disciples remembered that He said this," that is, "when He was raised from the dead . . ." The resurrection, among other things, triggered the memories of these disciples. Note second what "this" of "He said this" refers to. It refers to what Jesus said as recorded in verse 19, where we read, "Destroy this temple, and in three days I will raise it up." Note third John's comment about what Jesus said. "But He was speaking of the temple of His body" (John 2:21). Note fourth that "they believed the Scripture and the word which Jesus had spoken" (John 2:22). The "Scripture and the word which Jesus had spoken" are not the same thing. The "word which Jesus had spoken" is recorded in John 2:19. The Scripture must refer to the Old Testament. The disciples were interpreting the Old Testament, not only during the ministry of our Lord, but also after his resurrection and prior to the writing of the New Testament (and surely during and after its writing). The resurrection became an interpretive event through which the early disciples "believed the Scripture and the word which Jesus had spoken." Just as they began connecting the dots during our Lord's life-unto-death sufferings (John 2:17), so they continued to connect the dots when he entered into his glory, his resurrection (John 2:22; Cf. John 12:16 for the same phenomenon with reference to connecting the dots between our Lord and the book of Zechariah.).

Though it is true that we interpret the Bible in our day, it is also true that the early Christians interpreted the Bible of their day—i.e., the Old Testament. Some of their interpretations made it into the New Testament, as illustrated above. Though this does not mean that all of their personal interpretations of the Old Testament reflected the divine intention of the ancient text, it does mean that their interpretations recorded in the New Testament and affirmed by the authors of the New Testament (e.g., John) are infallible interpretations,[43] reflecting the intention of God who first gave the text. This is so because "All Scripture [i.e., Old and New Testament]

---

[43] This is not the same as claiming they were infallible interpreters.

is inspired by God" (2 Tim. 3:16) and inspiration implies infallibility.

It is obvious that interpreters of Scripture today have an advantage over the first-century interpreters mentioned above. We have God's own interpretation of the historical sufferings and glory of Christ—our New Testaments. But I think there is a good lesson for us to learn from the discussion above. When our Lord Jesus was on this earth, the Spirit of God was causing the disciples of Christ to recall texts of Scripture due to the presence and ministry of Christ. What their musings on the Old Testament contained in the New Testament show us is that the Old Testament points to Christ. The early disciples saw this more and more as they contemplated our Lord and the Old Testament. The inspired documents of the New Testament confirm that they were right. Not only was Jesus Christ the promised One, he was that to which the Old Testament pointed. The early disciples did not reinterpret the Old Testament in light of Christ; they interpreted it as pointing to Christ. And our New Testament is God's confirmation that they were right to do so. If it was right for them to do so, then it is right for us to do the same. The Old Testament is not about Christ simply because the New Testament says so. It is about Christ because that was God's intention from the beginning. This is how the early Christians (and our Lord) read the Old Testament. This is how we ought to as well.

Concluding Thoughts on Christ as *Scopus Scripturae*

An attempt has been made to display that Christ as *scopus Scripturae* is a concept attested in the Reformed tradition. It is present in Reformation and post-Reformation Reformed literature. It is clearly illustrated in John Owen and Nehemiah Coxe. Christ as *scopus Scripturae,* according to the Reformed, is a result of the exegesis of Scripture and the resultant identity of the target of all its parts.

We have also sought to display that this concept predates the Reformed confessions and theologians. Indeed, what has been argued is that it was the view of our Lord himself. Our Lord Jesus Christ understood his identity and vocation in light of our Old Testament and he saw it as a collective arrow pointing to him in his sufferings and glory (Luke 24:25-27, 44-47). It is clear from the writings of the New Testament that the Apostles utilized the same hermeneutical principles used by our Lord (cf. Luke 24:25-27, 44-47 and John 5:39, 45-47 with Matt. 2:13-15; Acts 2:14-36; 3:17-26; 9:1-19[44]; 15:12-19; 26:22-23; Rom. 5:14; 1 Pet. 1:10-12). It is also clear that the principles which led to the interpretive conclusion that Christ is the scope of the Old Testament predate our Lord. The principles that he utilized were not invented in the first century. They were applied in the first century though predating it.

What is more interesting, maybe even perplexing to some, is that Jesus and the authors of the New Testament give ample testimony that the authors of the Old Testament possessed a Messianic consciousness reflected in their writings (e.g., Luke 24:25-27, 44-47; John 5:39, 45-47; Acts 2:30-31; 3:21-26; 26:22-23; 1 Pet. 1:10-12). In other words, the New Testament sees the Old Testament as a Messianic document on its own terms. This is the divine commentary on the scope of the Old Testament. James Hamilton claims, ". . . from start to finish, the OT is a messianic document, written from a messianic perspective, to sustain a messianic hope."[45] I think he is right. He goes on to offer two caveats to this claim.

> First, I wish to make plain the inductive steps that led to this hypothesis. We inductively observe that there is much messianic speculation in second temple Judaism (both in the NT and the intertestamental literature). We add to this the observation that this speculation is anchored in the OT. We then set aside the possibility that ancient people were stupid, which seems to be an implicit assumption of a good deal of modern scholarship, and we seek a hypothesis that explains the data. Since the authors of these texts are presumably seeking to be persuasive to their contemporaries (see, e.g., John 20:31), it seems to me unlikely that

---

44 Cf. Seyoon Kim, *The Origin of Paul's Gospel* (1981; reprint, Eugene, OR: Wipf and Stock Publishers, 2007), where Kim argues that Paul's hermeneutic was permanently altered on the Damascus road.

45 James Hamilton, "The Skull Crushing Seed of the Woman: Inner-Biblical Interpretation of Genesis 3:15," *The Southern Baptist Journal of Theology* 10.2 (2006): 30.

their contemporaries would grant the imposition of new meanings onto these texts. One hypothesis that explains the fact that "Early Christians, rabbinic sources, and the sectarians at Qumran cite the same biblical texts in their portrayals of the royal messiah" (J. J. M. Roberts, "The Old Testament's Contribution to Messianic Expectations," in *The Messiah* [ed. J. H. Charlesworth; Minneapolis: Fortress, 1992], 41 n. 2) is that the OT is a messianic document, written from a messianic perspective, to sustain a messianic hope. This would mean that these disparate groups are not *imposing* a messianic interpretation on these texts but rightly interpreting them. This is not the only available hypothesis, but it seems to me to be the most convincing. I agree with John Sailhamer, who writes, "I believe the messianic thrust of the OT was the *whole* reason the books of the Hebrew Bible were written. In other words, the Hebrew Bible was not written as the national literature of Israel. It probably also was not written to the nation of Israel as such. It was rather written, in my opinion, as the expression of the deep-seated messianic hope of a small group of faithful prophets and their followers" ("The Messiah and the Hebrew Bible," *Journal of the Evangelical Theological Society* 44 [2001]: 23). The variations in messianic expectation show that the developing portrait of the coming Messiah was not crystal clear, but the pervasive expectation supports the hypothesis.

My second caveat is that though I am calling this "messianic," I do recognize that this term seems not to receive a technical meaning until the second temple period. But as Rose has written, "It is a matter of confusing language and thought . . . to conclude on this basis that one can speak of messianic expectations properly only after a particular word was used to refer to the person at the center of these expectations" (W. H. Rose, "Messiah," in *Dictionary of the Old Testament: Pentateuch* [Downers Grove: InterVarsity, 2003], 566). Cf. also John J. Collins, *The Scepter and the Star: The Messiahs of the Dead Sea Scrolls and Other Ancient Literature* (New York: Doubleday, 1995), 11–12.[46]

What Hamilton says of the Old Testament is agreed upon by all evangelicals concerning the New Testament. No one denies that the New Testament's scope is the coming, ministry, sufferings, and

[46] Hamilton, "The Skull Crushing Seed of the Woman," 44, n.5.

glory of Christ, along with the implications of these events drawn out and applied to the life of the early church. But our study presents a challenge to view the entirety of Scripture as finding its target or scope as our Lord Jesus Christ. Though it is true that neither Testament was intended by God to stand on its own, it is also true that the Old Testament, while it was on its own, witnessed to Christ, contained the saving knowledge of Christ, and produced believers in Christ. The same could be said of the New Testament, except that it never stood on its own. Since the documents that contained the promise of Christ had as its scope the person and office of the Messiah, then certainly the documents that contain the fulfillment in Christ do the same. Christ, then, is the target, the goal, the scope of the Scriptures, which give all glory to God.

PRAEDICATIO VERBI DEI EST VERBUM DEI: "The Preaching of the Word of God is the Word of God" – Heinrich Bullinger and The *Second Helvetic Confession*[1]

Ronald Baines*

The declaration "The Preaching of the Word of God is the Word of God" comes from the *Second Helvetic Confession* (*SHC*; Lat., *Confessio Helvetica Posterior*.[2] The original title was *Confessio et Expositio Simplex Orthodoxae Fidei*.).[3] This Confession was written by Heinrich Bullinger in 1562, apparently as a last bequest to the city of Zurich.[4]

---

* Ronald Baines is pastor of Grace Reformed Baptist Church, Brunswick, ME. He received the MAR from Reformed Theological Seminary and is a Ph.D. candidate at the University of Maine.

[1] Of the numerous editions available on the internet I have used the readily available electronic edition of the *Second Helvetic Confession* found in, *The Constitution of the Presbyterian Church (U. S. A.): Part 1 : Book of Confessions* (Louisville: Office of the General Assembly Presbyterian Church (U.S.A.), 1999), 51-116. Schaff calls the *Second Helvetic Confession* "the most catholic [universal] of the Swiss confessions." Philip Schaff, rev. David Shaff, *The Creeds of Christendom* (1931; reprint, Grand Rapids: Baker Book House, 1983), 3:233. Schaff provides only the Latin edition, referring the reader elsewhere for an English translation. A slightly edited English version can be found in James T. Dennison, Jr., comp., *Reformed Confessions of the 16th and 17th Centuries in English Translation: Volume 2, 1552-1566* (Grand Rapids: Reformation Heritage Books, 2010), 809-81.

[2] Richard A. Muller, *Dictionary of Latin and Greek Theological Terms: Drawn Principally from Protestant Scholastic Theology* (Grand Rapids: Baker Book House, 1985), 237.

[3] Edward A. Dowey Jr., "The Word of God as Scripture and Preaching" in W. Fred Graham, *Later Calvinism: International Perspectives, Sixteenth Century Essays & Studies* (Kirksville, Mo.: Sixteenth Century Journal Publishers, 1994), 5. This title can be found in the Latin edition reproduced by Schaff, *The Creeds of Christendom*, 3:233.

[4] Some authors suggest the composition of this Confession to be 1561, while others claim 1562. I have not done a detailed study in order to claim validity for either date. Due to his careful scholarship, I have opted to use Richard Muller's assertion of 1562. Cf. Richard A. Muller, *Post-Reformation Reformed Dogmatics: The Rise and Development of Reformed Orthodoxy, ca. 1520 to ca. 1725*, 2nd ed., 4 vols.

Heinrich Bullinger was born in the Swiss village of Bremgarten on July 18, 1504. His father was a parish priest who embraced the Reformation in 1529 (approximately seven years after his son) and subsequently married Bullinger's mother. Though their relationship began outside of the legal bonds of marriage, Heinrich's father, for whom he was named, had been a faithful husband and a good father.[5]

The younger Heinrich completed his education at the University of Cologne, achieving the master's degree. In 1522 he was converted and embraced the Reformation which necessitated a change in his future plans as the priesthood for which he was training was no longer an option. In spite of his Protestant leanings, Bullinger was invited to teach the monks at the Cistercian monastery of Kappel in the canton of Zurich. It was during this fruitful tenure that he became acquainted with Ulrich Zwingli, meeting for the first time in 1523. On the tragic death of Zwingli in 1531, the 27 year old Bullinger was chosen his successor as *antistes*, the minister of the famed Grossmunster church of Zurich. Steinmetz notes:

> On December 9, 1531, he stepped for the first time into the pulpit Zwingli had occupied with such distinction. Before he finished his first sermon, people realized that they had called a worthy successor to assume the leadership of the church of Zurich.[6]

He would remain in Zurich the rest of his life preaching as many as six sermons a week, writing some 12,000 letters and numerous theological treatises, and playing a pivotal role in the progress and success of the Reformation in Switzerland and beyond. Steinmetz asserts, "the degree of his influence on the course of the

---

(Grand Rapids: Baker Academic, 2003), 2:71, *PRRD* hereinafter. For a date of 1561 see, *The Constitution of the Presbyterian Church (U. S. A.): Part 1 : Book of Confessions*, 52.

[5] For the biographical details recounted here I am indebted to David C. Steinmetz, *Reformers in the Wings: From Geiler von Kaysersberg to Theodore Beza*, 2nd. Ed., (New York: Oxford Univ. Press, 2001), 93-99; and Machiel A. Van Den Berg, *Friends of Calvin* (Grand Rapids: Wm. B. Eerdmans Pub. Co., 2009), 217-26.

[6] Steinmetz, *Reformers in the Wings*, 97.

Reformation outside his native Switzerland has not yet been adequately assessed." He died in 1575 at the age of 71.[7]

Though written in 1562, the *SHC* became public in 1566 when Bullinger circulated it among the Reformed churches for the purpose of aiding the defense of Frederick III the elector of the Palatine. Because Frederick left the Lutherans, he was "summoned before the imperial diet in 1566 to defend his church against the charge that it fell outside the protection of the Peace of Augsburg."[8] Frederick was acquitted at the diet and the door opened for greater reformation among the churches of Germany. The *SHC* became one of the most widely accepted Confessions of the Reformation, finding acceptance in France, Switzerland, Scotland, and Hungary.[9]

The Statement's Place within the Confession

It is essential at the outset to place this important theological proposition within the context of the *SCH* before examining it in greater historical and theological detail. The Confession contains thirty Articles beginning with the doctrine of the Word under the heading *Of the Holy Scripture Being the True Word of God,* and concluding with Article XXX, *Of the Magistracy.* It contains articles that we would consider standard fare among Reformed churches and reflecting the now standard *loci* of systematic theology from the Word, God, Man (created and fallen), Christ, Salvation, the Church and its Sacraments. There are included within these Articles, however, subjects that might surprise us, such as the manner of burial and caring for the dead (Article 26) and the management of church possessions (Article 28).

It is imperative to observe that the proposition, *The Preaching of the Word of God is the Word of God,* is not found under the heading *Of the Catholic and Holy Church of God, and of the One Only Head of the*

---

[7] Steimetz, *Reformers in the Wings*, 99. Van Den Berg notes, ". . . it appears that Bullinger's published sermons had even more influence in England than the writings of Calvin." Cf. Van Den Berg, *Friends of Calvin*, 221.

[8] Philip Benedict, *Christ's Churches Purely Reformed: A Social History of Calvinism* (New Haven, CT: Yale University Press, 2002), 212-13.

[9] Benedict, *Christ's Churches Purely Reformed*, 57.

Church (Article 17), or under the articulation *Of the Ministers of the Church, Their Institution and Duties* (Article 18). Rather, it occurs as the heading of the fourth paragraph of the very first Article, *Of the Holy Scripture Being the True Word of God*.[10]

The importance of this placement cannot be overstated. The theological proposition is not so much about the dynamic of preaching, although it addresses that issue, but the long standing argument with late medieval Roman Catholicism about the very nature of the Word of God itself. In this light this essay seeks to assess Bullinger's declaration from within the discipline of historical theology. We will focus first on Bullinger's view of the Reformers in relation to the history of the Christian Church. Was the Reformation an innovation or a reclamation? We will then take up three changes that arose during medieval Roman Catholicism that Bullinger's *Confession* in general and this statement in particular counter. These are, first, the shift from Word to sacrament as the effectual instrument in salvation; second, the shift in hermeneutics from the plain interpretation of the Word to the medieval *quadriga*, the fourfold sense of the Word; and third, the shift within the church from the preaching of the Word as the primary focus of the pastoral office to the priestly exercise of sacramentalism as the means whereby grace is conferred within the context of the liturgy of the church. We will conclude with some present day application drawn from this important declaration.

From Ancient Faith to Medieval Superstition

In his earlier work of 1537 titled *Der Alt Gloub* (translated into English by Myles Coverdale as *The Old Faith*, in 1547), Bullinger addressed his response to the claim by Romanists that the Reformers were innovators. The issue is important because it allows us to determine if the *SHC* is to be viewed as simply a statement

---

10 The paragraph title in Latin is *Praedicatio Verbi Dei est Verbum Dei*. In the Latin edition of 1566 published in Zurich it appears in the margin next to the paragraph. Heinrch Bullinger, *Confessio et expositio simplex orthodoxae fidei & dogmatum Catholicorum syncerae religionis Christianae*, (Zurich: C. Froschower, 1566), 7.

regarding the sixteenth-century theological context of Reformed thinking or whether Bullinger, and those adopting the *SHC* so widely, viewed it as an expression of the faith once delivered to the saints. To this end, Bullinger notes:

> Of this then followed farther, that the singleness of faith was forgotten, new laws made, the old rites and customs either perverted, or else utterly overthrown and abused; whereby men came far from the doctrine and christian ceremonies, from the way of truth into error foolishly, and partly into ceremonies of idolatry. . . . And though this papistical religion hath endured, prevailed, and triumphed certain hundred years, yet hath God alway sent his faithful servants, and had a little holy flock of his own, like as afore time in the days of the Judges, of the kings of Judah and Israel, and in the captivity of Babylon, though it was almost at the worst afore and at the coming of Christ . . . all his bragging aside, let us cast his religion from us, and take upon us unfeignedly the true old religion, which hath endured since the beginning of the world by the which all the holy men have ever loved, worshipped, and served God, and knew nothing utterly of the pope's religion.[11]

Cornelis Venema's conclusions are fully warranted:

> As its title and subtitle indicate, Bullinger's aim in this work was to demonstrate that the Christian faith was as old as the world, and that the Reformation understanding of the faith was nothing more than a rediscovery of its truth. Contrary to the Roman Catholic objection that the Reformers were innovators, Bullinger insists in this treatise that the Reformation represented the rediscovery and restoration to its proper place of the old faith, which had been abandoned in significant measure by the innovations and inventions of medieval Catholicism.[12]

---

[11] Heinrich Bullinger, "The Old Faith" in Miles Coverdale et al., *Writings and Translations of Myles Coverdale* (Cambridge, UK: Printed at the University press, 1844), 82-83.

[12] Cornelis P. Venema, "Heinrich Bullinger's Der Alt Gloub ("The Old Faith"): An Apology for the Reformation" in *Mid-America Journal of Theology,* No. 15 (2004): 17-18. Muller fully concurs with Venema in this assessment: "Moreover, in all three of his more or less systematic works Bullinger was intent upon demonstrating both

In the fullest sense, Bullinger turned the accusation on its head: Catholicism was guilty of innovation, not the Reformers. We turn now to look at three of those innovations.

Three Changes

It is vital to see Bullinger's proposition "The Preaching of the Word of God is the Word of God," in the *SHC* in light of three fundamental changes that had taken place in the life and history of the church over the previous centuries. In essence, we must see Bullinger as responding to the innovations of medieval Romanism on the one hand and the Radical Reformation on the other.[13] These changes, while differing in nature between Romanism and Anabaptist radicalism, nonetheless touch the same three areas of innovation.

1. The normative foundation of the written Word of God

Medieval Romanism had essentially replaced the normativity of Scripture with the presumed authority of the *magisterium;* the teaching authority of the church. In so doing, the Scriptures were subordinated to the Roman church and coordinate with their declared canon of tradition. In the words of Joel Beeke, the medieval Roman church had successfully engineered the "Captivity

---

in principle and in specific doctrinal argument the continuity of the Reformation with the tradition of patristic interpretation and theology and, therefore, the catholicity of the Reformation. . . . Bullinger manifestly belongs to the interpretive model . . . where Scripture provides the absolute norm for doctrine and tradition remains a norm, but clearly subordinate to the biblical standard." Muller, *PRRD*, 2:72.

[13] That Bullinger was striking at errors in both Roman and Anabaptist views of Scripture's authority, necessity, and sufficiency is affirmed by W. Peter Stephens. Against both opponents, Stephens affirms, Bullinger insisted that the "Holy Spirit cannot be separated from Scripture, as the truth of God cannot be separated from God." Cf. W. Peter Stephens, "The Authority of the Bible in Heinrich Bullinger's Early Works" in *Reformation and Renaissance Review* 10, no. 1 (2008): 43, n. 26.

of the Word."[14] The Reformers set about to free the Word from this captivity and to restore it as the sole normative foundation for all of life and practice, thus the commonly known Reformed affirmation of *sola Scriptura*.

The Reformers affirmed that the authority of Scripture lies in its inspiration and is therefore the principle authority and the formal object of faith and revealed theology (*principium cognoscendi et obiectum formale fidei ac theologiae revelatae.*)[15] By affirming Scripture as the formal object of faith, Bullinger and the other Reformers were denying the Roman church's assertion that the sacraments have any operative power (*virtus operativa*) *ex opere operata* (by the work performed). The sacraments only communicate grace when they are accompanied by the Word preached.

In essence, Roman Catholicism taught saving grace was communicated through the sacramental system developed and canonized by the Roman church while the Reformers affirmed that they had no such power to communicate salvation but only became means of grace when faith was present. Bullinger affirmed that there was a direct relationship between the sacraments and the Word of God, especially as that Word is preached. But as Muller notes, the sacraments are a visible word (*verbum visiblis*) emphasizing their direct relationship to the Word of God.[16] Bullinger insists that the sacraments must be accompanied by the preaching of the Word and are simultaneously subordinate to the Word. The sacraments become a means of grace as they confirm the truths of the Word which have been embraced by faith, not because they somehow confer saving faith. Bullinger makes this point explicit in dealing with the relationship between the Word and the sacraments in his *Decades*.[17] He says:

---

[14] Joel Beeke, "The Origins of Calvinism" in Joel R. Beeke and Sinclair B. Ferguson, *Living for God's Glory: An Introduction to Calvinism* (Lake Mary, FL: Reformation Trust, 2008), 4.

[15] Muller, *Dictionary*, 52.

[16] Muller, *Dictionary*, 325.

[17] The *Decades* are a series of sermons Bullinger preached covering the whole range of biblical doctrine. The name derives from the fact that they were collected into five groups of ten sermons each. *The Decades* provide greater detail on

> The chief end of sacraments is this; that they are testimonies to confirm the truth, by which the Lord in his church even visibly doth testify, that the things now uttered by preaching of the gospel, and by the promises assured to the faithful from the beginning of the world, are in every point so brought to pass, and are so certainly true, as they are declared and promised in the word of truth.[18]

Furthermore, while the Reformers affirmed the freedom of God to work outside of the ordinary means of grace, they also affirmed there was no foundation for the Radical Reformation's advocacy of direct illumination apart from the Word. Though God was free to work outside of means, he had not ordained to do so ordinarily. To affirm God's absolute power to affect all possibilities was not to open the door to denying God's ordained ordinary power which he clearly communicated to be found in the ordinary expression of the means of grace.

The importance of the Reformed emphasis on God's ordained power as distinct from his absolute power is directly related to the preaching of the Word. This is underscored in the *SHC* in the section immediately following that of the Preaching of the Word of God.

> INWARD ILLUMINATION DOES NOT ELIMINATE EXTERNAL PREACHING. For he that illuminates inwardly by giving men the Holy Spirit, the same one, by way of commandment, said unto his disciples, "Go into all the world, and preach the Gospel to the whole creation" (Mark 16:15). And so in Philippi, Paul preached the Word outwardly to Lydia, a seller of purple goods; but the Lord inwardly opened the woman's heart (Acts 16:14). And the same Paul, after a beautiful development of his thought, in Rom. 10:17 at length comes to the conclusion, "So faith comes from hearing, and hearing from the Word of God by the preaching of Christ."

Bullinger's theology than one finds in the *SHC* and offer rich commentary on the theology of the *Confession*.

[18] Heinrich Bullinger and Thomas Harding, *The Decades of Henry Bullinger*, 4 vols. (Cambridge, UK: Printed at the University Press, 1849), 4:316.

> At the same time we recognize that God can illuminate whom and when he will, even without the external ministry, for that is in his power; but we speak of the usual way of instructing men, delivered unto us from God, both by commandment and examples.[19]

Understanding the statement "The Preaching of the Word of God is the Word of God" requires the Reformation reclamation of the sole sufficiency of Scripture as the absolute norm for all of faith and practice. Any other normative standard makes the preaching of the Word secondary at best and unnecessary at worst. Neither Romanism nor Radicalism had the proper normative foundation and so both had aberrant views of the centrality of preaching in the life of the church.

2. The proper interpretation of the written Word of God

While the normativity of the Word is foundational to a right understanding of the task of preaching of the Word, preaching cannot stand alone apart from the proper interpretation of the Word. This is underscored in the *SHC* by the placement of *Article 2, Of Interpreting the Holy Scriptures, and of Fathers, Councils, and Traditions,* immediately after the first Article on the Word and before all other doctrinal formulations within it. First the normativity of the Word is affirmed and then its right interpretation is asserted.

The Word of God as a normative standard was not to be handled haphazardly or individualistically. As Bullinger asserts, "we do not allow all possible interpretations."[20] Therefore, this normative standard needs to be interpreted properly and faithfully in order for the faithful to be instructed and grounded in those truths handed down to them in the written Word.

---

[19] *The Constitution of the Presbyterian Church (U. S. A.): Part 1: Book of Confessions*, 54.

[20] *The Constitution of the Presbyterian Church (U. S. A.): Part 1: Book of Confessions*, 55.

To this end, Bullinger rejected the Roman church's practice of the medieval *quadriga*, the four-fold sense of the Word.[21] Instead, he affirmed:

> But we hold that interpretation of the Scripture to be orthodox and genuine which is gleaned from the Scriptures themselves (from the nature of the language in which they were written, likewise according to the circumstances in which they were set down, and expounded in the light of like and unlike passages and of many and clearer passages) and which agree with the rule of faith and love, and contributes much to the glory of God and man's salvation.[22]

It is not that the Reformers invented what we now commonly call the grammatico-historical interpretation of Scripture, they did not. Muller and Thompson are clear that the Reformers stood in a long line of interpreters who evidence an "increasing interest in both the text and its literal sense."[23] In this way they stood on the shoulders

---

21 Alistair McGrath gives an overview of the quadriga. "The basic principle underlying this approach is as follows. Scripture possesses a number of different senses. In addition to the literal sense, three non-literal senses could be distinguished: the allegorical, regarding what Christians are to believe; the tropological or moral, regarding what Christians are to do; and the anagogical, regarding what Christians were to hope for. The four senses of Scripture were thus the following: 1 The literal sense, whereby the text was taken at face value. 2 The allegorical sense, whereby certain passages of Scripture were interpreted so as to produce statements of doctrine. Those passages tended to be either obscure, or to have a literal meaning which was unacceptable, for theological reasons, to their readers. 3 The tropological or moral sense, whereby certain passages were interpreted to produce ethical guidance for Christian conduct. 4 The anagogical sense, whereby certain passages were interpreted to indicate the grounds of Christian hope, pointing toward the future fulfillment of the divine promises in the New Jerusalem." Cf. Alister E. McGrath, *Reformation Thought: An Introduction*, 4th ed. (Malden, MA ; Oxford: Wiley-Blackwell, 2012), 103-04.

22 *The Constitution of the Presbyterian Church (U. S. A.): Part 1: Book of Confessions*, 55.

23 Richard A. Muller and John L. Thompson, "The Significance of Precritical Exegesis: Retrospect and Prospect" in David Curtis Steinmetz, Richard A. Muller, and John Lee Thompson, *Biblical Interpretation in the Era of the Reformation: Essays Presented to David C. Steinmetz in Honor of His Sixtieth Birthday* (Grand Rapids; Cambridge: W.B. Eerdmans, 1996), 344.

of a select body of medieval predecessors. It was not simply their affirmation of the *sensus literalis* or the *sensus historicus* that separated them from Roman Catholic interpreters. What was unique was that they limited themselves to an interpretive model that was scripturally defensible and defined. In other words, it was Scripture alone which gave them the foundation for limiting their interpretive practices to the literal sense, in its historical context, taken in light of the entire canonical corpus.

In the *First Decade*, the third sermon, Bullinger gives expression to this reality in summarizing the interpretive principles which marked the Reformers out from the Roman Catholics on the one hand and the Radical reformers on the other.

> But whereas the scripture doth admit an exposition, it doth not yet admit any exposition whatsoever: for that which savoureth of man's imagination it utterly rejecteth. For as by the Spirit of God the scripture was revealed, so by the same Spirit it is requisite to expound it. There are therefore certain rules to expound the word of God religiously by the very word of God itself: that is, so to expound it, that the exposition disagree not with the articles of our faith, nor be contrary to charity towards God and our neighbour; but that it be thoroughly surveyed, and grounded upon that which went before and followeth after, by diligent weighing of all the circumstances, and laying together of the places. And chiefly it is requisite, that the heart of the interpreter be godly bent, willing to plant virtue and pluck up vice by the roots, and finally, always ready evermore to pray to the Lord, that he will vouchsafe to illuminate our minds, that God's name may in all things be glorified. For his is the glory, honour, and dominion, for ever and ever. Amen.[24]

What is important to note in this summary, among other things, is Bullinger's assertion that the exegete not only requires the normative standard of the Word of God, the Spirit inspired text, but he is equally dependent upon the self-same Spirit to expound it truthfully and faithfully. This is critical for understanding more

---

[24] Bullinger and Harding, *The Decades of Henry Bullinger*, 1:80.

fully the proposition before us that "The Preaching of the Word of God is the Word of God." It is not any preaching, but preaching is only true preaching when the normative standard of the Word of God is expounded according the author's intent. And in this context, Bullinger affirms that the author is the Holy Spirit.[25]

What Bullinger did in the *SHC* was to make it impossible to assume that because "The Preaching of the Word of God is the Word of God," one could therefore adduce that preaching is the Word of God. The text and its interpretation are inseparably linked; the author of the one is the illuminator of the other.

3. The proper proclamation of the written Word of God

The final change which we shall consider in this short essay is the change in the task of the ministerial office. The change was both dramatic and detrimental to the life and health of the church. Malcolm Watts gives rich description to the changes that occurred during the medieval period.

> The Church of Rome degraded the Holy Scriptures by alloying the purity of the Canon with her apocryphal additions, by supplementing the inspired records with an enormous mass of spurious traditions, by admitting only that interpretation which is according to "the unanimous consent of the Fathers" and "the Holy Mother Church," and, particularly by diminishing the role of preaching as their "priests" busied themselves with miraculous stories about Mary, the saints and the images, and magnified the

[25] This is not a denial of the human author's intent, but an assertion that the meaning of the text is ultimately defined by the divine author not delimited by the human author. The critical methods that have developed since the Enlightenment have treated the biblical text like any other ancient document and have championed that the only intent one can consider is the human author's original intent. The challenge with this methodology is the denial of the relevance, if not the presence, of the divine author. For an insightful discussion of this distinction and the need to rethink the pre-critical interpretation of Scripture along the lines of the Reformers, see, David C. Steinmetz, "The Superiority of Pre-Critical Exegesis" in *Theology Today* 37, no. 1 (1980). I am indebted to Stefan Lindblad for helping me to understand this distinction more fully and for pointing me to Steinmetz's excellent article.

> importance of the Mass, with its elaborate and multiplied ceremonies and rituals. It was thus that preaching deteriorated and, in fact, almost disappeared. The Reformers vigorously protested against this and contended with all their might for the recovery of God's Holy Word.[26]

The importance of the recovery of the preaching of the Word as the most central task of the pastoral office cannot be overstated. When the preacher's voice was silenced in the churches, it must be understood that simultaneously the voice of God was rendered dumb as well.

It is the voice of God in the preached Word that gives full expression to the affirmation that "The Preaching of the Word of God is the Word of God." According to Edward A. Dowey Jr., this statement within the *SHC* "reflects a lifelong preoccupation of Bullinger with the *viva voce*."[27] The preaching of the Word of God is not a static or an academic exercise. It is a spiritually dynamic exercise that involves the right proclamation of the Word of God made living and vital by the Spirit acting to apply it savingly and sanctifyingly to the faithful hearers. As Muller aptly notes:

> Reformation and post-Reformation interpretation of Scripture, for all of its emphasis upon a strict grammatical reading of the text, holds in common with the earlier exegesis a sense of the direct address of the text to the present-day church. The preacher is not one who applies an old word to new situations, but rather he is a servant and an instrument of the living Word, the *viva Vox Dei*, for its effective operation in the world.[28]

It is because this living voice, which at first became the substance of the written Word, is still living that Bullinger can say, "For God

---

[26] As quoted in Beeke and Ferguson, *Living for God's Glory*, 4.

[27] Dowey, "The Word of God as Scripture and Preaching" in Graham, *Later Calvinism*, 9.

[28] Muller, *Dictionary*, 328.

himself spoke to the fathers, prophets, apostles, and still speaks to us through the Holy Scriptures."[29]

However, an important distinction needs to be made at this juncture. As has already been established, Bullinger and the Reformers considered the Word of God to be the sole foundational normative standard for all faith and practice. But is the voice of God which by inspiration gave the Word of God to the church the same voice of God to be heard in the preaching of the Word? In reality we need to see a distinction without a separation here.

Dowey, again, makes a careful distinction:

> The "outer" and "inner" modes through which the Spirit works are inseparably bound together, barring only the freedom of God to "illuminate whom and when he will" (223.47). Together they constitute the *usitata ratio* (224.49), the ordinary or normal way by which the Word comes to men. The "outer" elements are means or instruments, usually referred to with *per* (through), a preposition of agency. This is unmistakable in the Second Helvetic Confession, particularly in the passage that reads: But this faith is a pure gift of God, which God alone of his grace gives to his elect according to his measure when, to whom, and to the degree he wills. And he does this by the Holy Spirit by means of the preaching of the Gospel and steadfast prayer.[30]

In other words, the statement that "The Preaching of the Word of God is the Word of God" is not equating the normativity of the Word of God with the act of preaching. This would leave us with two normative standards. What Bullinger is affirming, rather, is the Word of God alone is normative, but that preaching is instrumentally the Word of God. As the normative Word of God is faithfully exegeted and proclaimed, the preaching of the Word becomes the instrumental means that the Holy Spirit uses as he causes the faithful to hear the very voice of God.

---

29 *The Constitution of the Presbyterian Church (U. S. A.): Part 1: Book of Confessions*, 53.

30 Dowey, "The Word of God as Scripture and Preaching" in Graham, *Later Calvinism*, 11.

In the fourth sermon of the *First Decade*, Bullinger explicates the connection of faith to the preached word.

> And yet we have to consider here, that God, in giving and inspiring faith, doth not use his absolute power, or miracles, in working; but a certain ordinary means agreeable to man's capacity: although he can indeed give faith without those means, to whom, when, and how it pleaseth him. But we read, that the Lord hath used this ordinary means even from the first creation of all things. Whom he meaneth to bestow knowledge and faith on, to them he sendeth teachers, by the word of God to preach true faith unto them. Not because it lieth in man's power, will, or ministry, to give faith; nor because the outward word spoken by man's mouth is able of itself to bring faith: but the voice of man, and the preaching of God's word, do teach us what true faith is, or what God doth will and command us to believe. For God himself alone, by sending his Holy Spirit into the hearts and minds of men, doth open our hearts, persuade our minds, and cause us with all our heart to believe that which we by his word and teaching have learned to believe.[31]

Greg Scharf confirms Bullinger's assertion that preaching is instrumentally the Word of God but not normatively the Word of God, when he says:

> This functional linkage between the two terms paves the way for an understanding of how preaching, including contemporary preaching, can be said to be the word of God. In preaching, the *function* of God exhorting his people is achieved, as long as the preacher does not depart from the *norm* of Scripture. "Scripture alone is the sufficient and authoritative norm also of preaching." That is, the link between Scripture and preaching whereby both can be referred to as the Word of God is instrumental, not normative. Preaching is not normative the way the Bible is.[32]

---

[31] Bullinger and Harding, *The Decades of Henry Bullinger*, 1:84-85.

[32] Greg R. Scharf, "Was Bullinger Right About the Preached Word" in *Trinity Journal* 26, No. 1 (2005): 5.

Conclusion

The Reformation acted as a counter to two very divergent currents with respect to the Word of God. Romanism subordinated the normative standard of Scripture to the Roman church, while the Radical Reformation substituted private illumination as the normative standard for all faith and practice. As a result, the process of interpretation became institutionalized within the *magisterium* of the Roman church entirely separating the pastoral office from the preaching function of the local church.[33] Additionally the Roman church canonized tradition and added layers of interpretation which obscured the perspicuous Word in multiple ways, while the Radical Reformation effectively rejected the need for textual interpretation within the context of the church locally or historically. Finally, both had a profound effect on the task of preaching. As the Roman church eliminated the necessity of preaching the Word to the faithful, grace was, it was claimed, communicated apart from the Word through the sacramental system of Rome. The Radical Reformation pretended to accomplish the same end by eliminating the means of grace communicated through the preached Word and settling for private immediate revelation of the Holy Spirit.

By restoring the Word of God to its rightful place as the sole normative standard for all of faith and practice and the preaching of the Word of God as the ordained instrumental means of communicating the normative Word to the faithful, the living, active voice of God was restored to the church. The *SHC* reflects this succinctly and eloquently in the phrase "The Preaching of the Word of God is the Word of God."

As an appropriate conclusion to our study, it behooves us to ask what implications this might have for us today. Greg Scharf

---

33 For the Roman Church's distinction of the teaching church from the learning church (*ecclesia docens from the ecclesia discens*) and the Reformers categorical rejection of this distinction, see Muller, *Dictionary*, 100.

provides six very pointed and helpful implications worthy of consideration.

1. If the preaching of the word of God is the word of God, then we who lead churches should make sure that preaching has the prominent, central place among the means God has given to make his nature and will known and to achieve his purposes for the church. Other means have their place, but what can compare with hearing the voice of God that we may live?
2. If the preaching of the word of God is the word of God, then those who preach should spare no effort to make sure that what they preach conforms to the content, tone, and purposes of the written word of God. That is, the sermon should be faithful not only to the passage being expounded but also to the immediate and extended literary context in which it is found.
3. If preaching the word of God is the word of God then we who preach should expect God's voice to be heard when we preach. To expect less is to settle for something less than God intends.
4. If the preaching of the word of God is the word of God, then those who speak on God's behalf should anticipate that God's word will go to work in those who hear it as such. Because God's word is living and active, the force of the teaching, correction, and rebuking it undertakes are God's work through us, not merely our work to achieve his purposes. We preach in hope.
5. If the preaching of the word of God is the word of God, then the triumph of his word in its work in listeners defines success in preaching, not how hearers rate the preacher. This fact does not excuse ethical carelessness, as 1 Thess 2:1–12 makes plain, but it does free us from *reliance upon* our rhetorical skills (1 Cor 2:1–5).
6. If the preaching of the word of God is the word of God then those who hear the word preached should take it as seriously as they would if God were speaking *directly* to them. Our hearers should listen expectantly and soberly and do what God asks them to do. They should say with Cornelius, "Now

we are all here in the presence of God to listen to everything the Lord has commanded you to tell us" (Acts 10:33).[34]

[34] Scharf, "Was Bullinger Right About the Preached Word" in *Trinity Journal*, 26, No. 1, (2005): 9-10.

SUFFICIENT, CERTAIN, AND INFALLIBLE:

The Inscripturated Word

James M. Renihan*

In his extremely helpful *Dictionary of Latin and Greek Theological Terms,* Richard A. Muller comments on the central role Scripture plays in the formulation of Christian theology. He states:

> [T]he *principium cognoscendi,* the principle of knowing or cognitive foundation, is a term applied to Scripture as the noetic or epistemological *principium theologiae,* without which there could be no true knowledge of God and therefore no theological system.[1]

Orthodox post-Reformation theologians would concur without dissent. The only saving means of knowing God is through the revelation he has given of himself.

This is the context out of which the Second London Confession (2LCF) of Particular or Reformed Baptists was born. Believing that God's purpose for humanity required a sufficient, certain, and infallible word from God, they identified this word as the 'Scripture of Truth' (a common phrase used to refer to the Bible) and set about building a system of theology from its materials. Our task in this article is simply to notice and understand how they began to form these divine resources into a cohesive whole. We shall do so by examining the first paragraph of the 2LCF.

---

* James M. Renihan is Dean and Professor of Historical Theology at the Institute of Reformed Baptist Studies in Escondido, CA. This material is from his forthcoming exposition of the Second London Confession of Faith.

[1] Richard A. Muller, *Dictionary of Latin and Greek Theological Terms: Drawn Principally from Protestant Scholastic Theology* (Grand Rapids: Baker Book House, 1985), 246. This dictionary is a *sine qua non* for study of post-Reformation confessions of faith.

Chapter 1 Of the Holy Scriptures

Paragraph 1. *The Holy Scripture is the only sufficient, certain, and infallible rule of all saving Knowledge, Faith and Obedience; Although the light of Nature, and the works of Creation and Providence do so far manifest the goodness, wisdom and power of God, as to leave men unexcusable; yet are they not sufficient to give that knowledge of God and His will, which is necessary unto Salvation. Therefore it pleased the Lord at sundry times, and in divers manners, to reveal himself, and to declare that His will unto his Church; and afterward for the better preserving, and propagating of the Truth, and for the more sure Establishment, and Comfort of the Church against the corruption of the flesh, and the malice of Satan, and of the World, to commit the same wholly unto writing; which maketh the Holy Scriptures to be most necessary, those former ways of Gods revealing his will unto his people being now ceased.*

1. General comments on the first sentence

The first part of the initial sentence of this paragraph, *The Holy Scripture is the only sufficient, certain, and infallible rule of all saving Knowledge, Faith and Obedience,* is not found in the two direct source documents of 2LCF, the Westminster Confession of Faith (WCF) or the Savoy Declaration (SD) and has been added by the Baptists.[2] While they may have simply wished to fortify their statement on Scripture, there are at least three possible reasons for the addition, although each of them may have together contributed to the desire to begin the Confession with these words. The first reason has reference to the Quakers. Michael A. G. Haykin has said, "It is very probable that this strengthening of the statement on Scripture grew out of the Particular Baptist concern with the Quakers . . . ."[3] Robert Oliver states that the influential Broadmead Church in Bristol "lost

[2] On the sources of the major seventeenth-century Baptist Confessions, see James M. Renihan, *True Confessions: Baptist Documents in the Reformed Family* (Owensboro, KY: RBAP, 2004).

[3] Michael A. G. Haykin, "The 1689 Confession: A Tercentennial Appreciation," unpublished paper dated 26 June 1990, 12.

a quarter of its members to the Quakers" in the mid 1650s.[4] In the manuscript records of the Petty France Church we find this entry for 8 October 1676, 10 months before the Confession is first mentioned in the same book:

> Mrs. Hattam was cut off from this congregation for forsaking the assembly of this and all other churches of Christ, and closing in with and cleaving to the Quakers: of whose evils she had often been admonished, both by the elders, brethren, and also appointment of the congregation, who divers times sent messengers to endeavor the reclaiming of her, but she neglected, and refused to hear them and therefore was she thus proceeded against according to the rule of Christ.[5]

Such inroads would certainly influence the Baptists as they prepared a new Confession. An opening sentence asserting the central role of Scripture in the church would immediately alert readers to the Baptist churches' commitment to the centrality of Scripture.

The second factor which may have contributed to the change was the fear of Roman Catholicism. Charles II issued a Declaration of Indulgence in March 1672 which granted a certain amount of freedom to the dissenters, but it also allowed Roman Catholics to gather for worship in private homes. This lifting of the proscription against Roman Catholics was not happily received by the dissenters, who feared that the benefits of the Reformation might be slowly slipping away. Many of these Baptists knew of the struggles of Protestants in Roman Catholic countries, such as France, and did not want to find themselves in a similar situation. As such, it was beneficial to strengthen their statement to speak of the exclusive rule of faith, which is the Scripture. This is not to say that a

---

[4] Robert G. Oliver, "Baptist Confession Making 1644 and 1689," unpublished paper presented to the Strict Baptist Historical Society, March, 1989, 12. In 1657, Robert Purnell, elder in the Broadmead. Bristol church published *The Church of Christ in Bristol Recovering Her Vail* (London: Thomas Brewster) as part of a controversy with Quakers that had erupted in his church. Dennis Hollister, an elder, had abandoned the church to go off to the Quakers, taking many with him.

[5] "Petty France Church Minute Book," October, 1676.

supplement such as this would prevent the political return of the power of the Roman church, but rather that such a return would diminish the place of Scripture in English theology.[6]

A third factor which may have contributed to the change was the theological argumentation of their paedobaptist brothers. Jack Rogers and Donald Mckim, in their book *The Authority and Interpretation of the Bible: An Historical Approach*, describe an intriguing line of reasoning put forward by Cornelius Burges, an important member of the Westminster Assembly. They state "Cornelius Burges used the covenant theme polemically against the Anabaptists . . ." Burgess argued that the broad analogy of Scripture supports paedobaptism, and that it is permitted "notwithstanding that no text of Scripture enjoyne it in so many words."[7] It is very possible that the Baptist response to this line of argument was to fortify their Confession by adding these words. In light of the modification made in 1:6,[8] this is perhaps the most likely reason for the addition here. Having said this, any or all of these factors may have led to the desire to begin their document with this assertion. The rest of the paragraph is identical to both SD and the WCF.

It is useful to note that this first sentence incorporates ideas contained in the second and third questions of the *Westminster Shorter Catechism*:

> *Q. What rule hath God given to direct us how we may glorify and enjoy him?*

---

[6] Benjamin Keach suggests this when he says "If the Scripture be not the Word of God, then God hath left us no certain rule at all, either of faith or practice; nor is there any way for us to know truth from error. The Papists say, the Church is the rule." Benjamin Keach, *An Exposition of the Parables*, (London: Aylott, 1858 reprint), 852.

[7] Jack B. Rogers and Donald K. McKim, *The Authority and Interpretation of the Bible: An Historical Approach* (San Francisco: Harper, 1979), 215.

[8] See James M. Renihan, "'Good and Necessary Consequences' or 'Necessarily Contained': A Particular Baptist Method of Theology" in Richard Barcellos, ed., *Southern California Reformed Baptist Pastors' Conference Papers: Volume 1, 2012* (Palmdale, RBAP, 2013), 129-52.

A. The Word of God (which is contained in the Scriptures of the Old and New Testament) is the only rule to direct us how we may glorify and enjoy him.

Q. What do the Scriptures principally teach?

A. The Scriptures principally teach, What man is to believe concerning God, and what duty God requires of man.[9]

These two questions and their answers provide a backdrop to the Baptist addition. A high view of the nature of Scripture was a commonplace among the English theologians. Certainly the prominence given to this phrase, on the very threshold of the 2LCF, demonstrates its importance.

2. Analysis of the first sentence

The basic teaching of the statement is this: *The Holy Scripture is the . . . rule.* But what does this mean? The sentence should be read something like this:

	sufficient		knowledge
The Holy Scripture is the only	certain	rule of all saving	faith
	and infallible		and obedience.

The *rule* is Scripture, and Scripture is the rule. The *Oxford English Dictionary*[10] (*OED*) gives some help in understanding the choice of this word when it provides the sense, "A standard of discrimination or estimation; a criterion, test, canon." The Scriptures are a judge, a standard, a criterion. Thomas Watson said "the Word is a rule of faith, a canon to direct our lives. . . . The Scripture is a full and perfect canon, containing in it all things necessary to salvation."[11] It speaks to life, and in doing so, gives authoritative wisdom. It has a

---

[9] *The Westminster Standards: An Original Facsimile* (Audubon, NJ: Old Paths Publications, 1997 facsimile reprint of 1648 edition), spelling updated.

[10] The *Oxford English Dictionary (OED)* is a very useful tool for defining terms according to their use in various periods of the history of the English language. Every serious student of the Confession must employ it.

[11] Thomas Watson, *A Body of Practical Divinity* (London: 1692), 15.

special authority and serves as the highest test for life. Notice how the word is used elsewhere in 2LCF:

> 1:2 All which are given by the inspiration of God, to be the **rule** of Faith and Life;
>
> 19:2 "The same Law that was first written in the heart of man, continued to be a perfect **rule** of Righteousness after the fall;
>
> 19:6 Although true *Believers* be not under the Law, as a Covenant of *Works*, to be thereby Justified or condemned; yet it is of great use to them as well as to others: in that, as a **Rule** of *Life*, informing them of the Will of *God*, and their Duty, it directs and binds them, to walk accordingly;
>
> 26:12 As all Believers are bound to joyn themselves to particular *Churches*, when and where they have opportunity so to do; So all that are admitted unto the priviledges of a *Church*, are also under the Censures and Government thereof, according to the **Rule** of *Christ*;
>
> 27:2 "the **rule** of the Gospel;
>
> *Appendix*, first sentence: Whosoever reads, and impartially considers what we have in our forgoing confession declared, may readily perceive, That we do not only concenter with all other true Christians on the Word of God (revealed in the Scriptures of truth) as the foundation and **rule** of our faith and worship.

Nehemiah Coxe, in an ordination sermon, states, "the wisdom of Christ saw it best to leave the churches to the Rule of his Written Word."[12] Clearly, the language means that the Scriptures are the standard for Christians. But notice that *rule* is modified by four adjectives: *only, sufficient, certain* and *infallible*. Each of these deserves some investigation.

---

12 N[ehemiah] C[oxe], *A Sermon at the Ordinatoin* [sic] *of an Elder and Deacons in a Baptized Congregation in London* (London: 1681), 17.

Only
This adjective modifies all three of those that follow: *only* sufficient, *only* certain, *only* infallible. It asserts a unique status for the Scriptures. In this chapter several potential modes of revelation recognized by different traditions are mentioned, and this word certainly anticipates each of them. They are: general revelation, personal revelation, the Apocrypha, new revelations of the Spirit, traditions of men, and private spirits.[13] Likewise, at other places in the Confession, other possible modes of revelation are mentioned, for example 'imaginations and devices of men" and "suggestions of Satan" in 22:1. None of these things can have the status of Scripture. The word "only" emphasizes the unique nature of the Scriptures. There are no other writings, or dreams, or Light of Christ[14] which may claim to have the religious authority of the written Word of God.

Sufficient
This term implies that Scripture includes every necessary teaching for man's saving knowledge, saving faith and saving obedience. There are other forms of revelation, but they are insufficient. There is, for example, the light of nature. Likewise, there are the works of creation and providence. But here at the outset is an assertion that these things, in and of themselves, do not and cannot reveal to men what they need for saving knowledge, saving faith, and saving obedience. The term, "sufficient" is defined in paragraph six of this first chapter, "The whole counsel of God concerning all things necessary for his own glory, man's salvation, faith and life, is either expressly set down or necessarily contained in the Holy Scripture: unto which nothing at any time is to be added, whether by new revelation of the Spirit, or traditions of men."

---

[13] L. Russ Bush and Tom J. Nettles, *Baptists and the Bible* (Nashville: Broadman & Holman,1999), 49.

[14] See Margery Post Abbott, Mary Ellen Chijoke, Pink Dandelion and John W. Oliver, Jr., *Historical Dictionary of the Friends (Quakers)* (Oxford: Scarecrow Press, 2003), 157.

Certain

L. Russ Bush and Tom Nettles state, "Those things declared in Scripture are found to occur or to have occurred exactly as represented."[15] The *OED* suggests several senses for this word:

> 1. Determined, fixed, settled; not variable or fluctuating; unfailing; 2. Sure, unerring, not liable to fail; to be depended upon; wholly trustworthy or reliable; 3. Established as a truth or fact to be absolutely received, depended, or relied upon; not to be doubted, disputed, or called into question; indubitable, sure.

Bush and Nettles again say:

> None of the statements of Scripture fails to represent reality accurately. This is the same idea that is properly conveyed by the word 'inerrant' as it is used in scholarly evangelical discussions today. 'Certain' refers only to the character of what is actually written. It affirms that nothing misleading or erroneous exists in Scripture.[16]

The term "certain," refers to that which is sure. When seeking to describe the content of the knowledge God possesses, the Confessions states in 2:2, "his knowledge is infinite, infallible, and independent upon the creature, so as nothing is to him contingent or uncertain." This negation helps to define the affirmation of the Confession's first sentence. Scripture is certain in that it is a faithful record of all that God intended to reveal. This is undoubtedly the meaning of the word as written by the Particular Baptists. Scripture is certain–i.e. it is inerrant.

Infallible

The fourth term, "infallible," is of great importance. William Estep points out that "it was . . . the first time in any Baptist Confession that the Bible was declared 'infallible.'"[17] Haykin states:

---

[15] Bush and Nettles, *Baptists*, 49.

[16] Bush and Nettles, *Baptists*, 49.

[17] William R. Estep, "Biblical Authority in Baptist Confessions of Faith, 1610-1963" in Robison B. James, ed., *The Unfettered Word: Southern Baptists Confront the Authority-Inerrancy Question* (Waco: Word Books, 1987), 169.

> Scripture is also 'infallible,' which is a far stronger term than 'certain' or 'inerrant.' To describe something as 'infallible' is not merely to assert that it does not err, but to maintain that it cannot err." Infallible strengthens certain, and belongs with it in just the same way that we speak of the Scriptures as "infallible and inerrant.[18]

The *OED* gives evidence of the fact that this word was used with this sense so far back as 1491 to refer to the impossibility of error.

In these ways, the Particular Baptists summarized their understanding of Scripture at the outset of their Confession. It is unique as a sufficient, certain, and infallible rule. But notice also the sphere of the rule: saving knowledge, saving faith, and saving obedience. To what do these things refer? It seems that we must see a certain difference in each of them. "Saving knowledge" is the doctrine necessary to know God as savior. The Baptists are not asserting that the Bible is the only source of any knowledge, but rather of saving knowledge. General revelation may tell us that there is a God, and reveal to us his power and eternal being, but it cannot tell us that he is merciful and saving. Special revelation—the Scriptures—are necessary for this. "Saving faith" is of course the apprehension of the gospel in conversion and throughout life on this earth, and "saving obedience" is its twin: repentance (see 2LCF 15).

But does this mean that the Baptists believed that the rule of Scripture did not extend to every area to which it spoke? As, for example, when it addresses science and history? Some Baptists have asserted this very thing. There are a few who would seek to limit these statements of authority to the areas of faith and practice. For example, William F. Lumpkin, in his article An "Appraisal of Intent in Baptist Statements of Biblical Authority" says:

> Questions of errancy of the Scriptures did not occupy the minds of those who prepared the Confessions. For the authors the Scriptures were infallible in their primary purpose—the glorification of God in man's salvation. In this area, they were

---

[18] Haykin, *Appreciation*, 12.

> perfect and sufficient. The Word of God has, indeed, other purposes than salvation; but these purposes are subordinate to and flow from the saving purpose of the Word. Therefore the 'infallibility' and truth of which the 17th and 18th century confessors spoke is not to be equated with the modern concept of inerrancy. To say that these men taught the inerrancy of Scripture because they did not assert that there are errors in Scripture is 'to impose a modern problem on a pre-scientific statement.' Like the Reformers before them, the Baptist confessors were entirely confident of the inspiration of the Scriptures and so were free to deal with critical questions. The question of errancy or inerrancy was one to which they were strangers. The great issue was the truth and infallibility of the Word for every soul who has 'tasted that the Word is precious.' Textual considerations were always of minor interest as compared with the central purpose of Scripture.[19]

James Leo Garrett, Jr. states, "The Second London . . . Confession . . . used the term 'infallible' to refer to the Bible's function as 'rule,' to the Bible's containing 'infallible truth,'" while others make similar limitations to the areas of "faith and practice." [20] But we should ask if this is a proper delimitation with regard to the statements of this Confession.

One specimen we may use to demonstrate that these men are reading the text incorrectly is the writings of the men who published the Confession. These seventeenth-century authors frequently refer to the "Scriptures of Truth," believing that they cannot lie. For one example, let's notice Benjamin Keach.[21] His

---

[19] William Lumpkin, "An Appraisal of Intent in Baptist Statements of Biblical Authority" in *Perspectives in Religious Studies*, 1 (1974) 163. The citation in the midst of the paragraph is from Jack Rogers, *Scripture in the Westminster Confession* (Kampen: J. H. Koh, 1966), 305.

[20] James Leo Garrett, Jr., "Biblical Authority According to Baptist Confessions of Faith," *Review and Expositor*, 76 (Winter 1979): 47-48 and J. William Angell, "The Place of Biblical Authority among Baptists," *Greek Orthodox Theological Review*, 22 (1977): 451.

[21] For information on Keach see Austin Walker, *The Excellent Benjamin Keach* (Dundas: Joshua Press, 2004) and D. B. Riker, *A Catholic Reformed Theologian:*

reputation as a leader among these Baptists is unchallenged, and he was involved in signing the 2LCF as a representative of his church at Horse-lie-Down, Southwark. In Book Four of his *Exposition of the Parables*, originally published in 1701, there is a series of sermons on Luke 16:19-31. Keach forthrightly describes his view of the full extent of the 'certainty' (i.e., inerrancy) of Scripture. He says:

> Argu. I. My first argument to prove the divine authority of the holy Scriptures shall be taken from the matter contained in them, and their sublime style: certainly this proves they are not of an human product, what writings carry in them or discover such amazing mysteries? 1. What human brain could have imagined a Trinity in the Godhead, or have given an account of the manner of God's existence . . . . 2. The holy scripture only gives an account of the beginning of the world, which men by natural light have given full demonstrations could not be from eternity, but had a beginning; but deny the holy scriptures to be true, or from God. *It is impossible for us to know how they were created, or how long since, or how long God was in creating of it, and all things that are therein; and can it be imagined that the holy God would keep mankind (for whom he made this world) ignorant of this important matter.*[22]

There can be no question but that Keach accepted the testimony of Scripture as true in all things. He says more:

> Argu. II. My second argument shall be taken from the antiquity of the Scriptures. . . . [I]f the Scripture be not of God, then Moses is a grand impostor, and the first religion a mere counterfeit, and that the devil set up his chapel before God built his church . . .
>
> Argu. III. Consider yet further, the credit and sincerity of the penman of sacred scriptures; for were they not what they pretend to be, viz., the Word of God, and *dictated to the writers therof by the Spirit of God,* it would be the greatest affront to the Divine Majesty imaginable, and the greatest cheats towards mankind, that ever was put upon the world.[23]

Federalism and Baptism in the Thought of Benjamin Keach, 1640-1704 (Portland, OR: Wipf and Stock, 2010).

[22] Keach, *Exposition,* 848, emphasis mine.

[23] Keach, *Exposition,* 849-50, emphasis mine.

In these words, Keach advocates a dictation theory of inspiration. While this is beyond the compass of the Confession, and modern evangelical and Reformed scholarship would eschew this theory, its presence in Keach's writings testifies to his understanding of the nature of biblical authority. He considered the Bible to be a book directly inspired by God in all of its facets. His sermons are fascinating, as they go on and on with pertinent arguments to demonstrate the truthfulness and authority of the Word of God. There is no doubt that when Keach, as a leader among the Particular Baptists, penned his name to the 2LCF, he understood that it taught that which he believed. Anything less would have made him into a hypocrite. In fact, there is no evidence to suggest that any of the other Particular Baptists considered the issue differently from Keach. While he may have been a man of his own age in the adoption of a dictation theory of inspiration as opposed to the better concursive theory, he nevertheless was one with modern Evangelicals who would hold to an inerrant and infallible Bible in every matter it addresses.

Having opened up the first sentence, let's proceed to examine the rest of the paragraph.

The Necessity of Scripture[24]

The first paragraph of the Confession focuses our attention on the necessity of Scripture. It teaches us several important things:

1. The reality and trustworthiness of natural revelation

> *Although the light of Nature, and the works of Creation and Providence do so far manifest the goodness, wisdom and power of God, as to leave men unexcusable . . .*

What is "the light of Nature"? In this clause, the light of nature is distinguished from and supplemented by the works of creation and

---

[24] I rely throughout the rest of this article on B. B. Warfield's outline of Chapter 1 found in *The Westminster Assembly and its Work* (1931; reprint, Grand Rapids: Baker Book House, 1981), 191-92.

providence. These later two external works of God are described in detail in chapters 4 and 5 of 2LCF, but the phrase 'light of nature' may be somewhat obscure. The expression appears three other times in the Confession: 1:6, 10:4, and 22:1. By comparing these three citations, we may see that it refers to general or natural revelation. But we must understand this in two ways: on the one hand, it is the general revelation that discloses to us the existence of God, and certain of his attributes. But on the other hand, it is more than that. It is also the things around us that we learn about the world and our existence based on our (humanity's) observations. It can teach us a great deal about the world, but it is limited in what it will teach us about God. It instructs us that God is good, wise, just, and powerful, but it gives us no further insight into the divine being. We cannot know him as Trinity, nor are we able to understand that he is a loving and gracious God. We simply know that he is good—he sends rain on the just and the unjust, that he orders his world to reveal knowledge (Psalm 19:2), and that he has power over all of the vast creation he has made. Nowhere, however, does general revelation tell us about the majestic and beautiful trinitarian being of God, nor of his redeeming love shown in Jesus Christ. This is why we need the Scriptures. Thus, as the Confession tells us, there is natural, or general revelation. It conveys to us some things about God, but only enough to condemn us—to leave us without excuse.

2. The insufficiency of natural revelation

> *. . . yet are they not sufficient to give that knowledge of God and His will, which is necessary unto Salvation.*

This natural revelation cannot save anyone. Though much more might be said, suffice that this was a disputed point among seventeenth-century Baptists. In General Baptist ranks, the notion of salvation by general revelation was commonplace.[25] For those

---

[25] See James M. Renihan, "'That Strong Hold of Their Common Faith:' Salvation in Christ Alone among Seventeenth-Century Baptists" in *Journal of the Institute of Reformed Baptist Studies* (2014): 69-94.

with Reformed convictions, the notion of salvation apart from the knowledge of Christ was unthinkable. Notice how the doctrine here is supplemented by Westminster Larger Catechism Question 60:

> Q. Can they who have never heard the gospel, and so know not Jesus Christ, nor believe in him, be saved by their living according to the light of nature?
> A: They who, having never heard the gospel, know not Jesus Christ, and believe not in him, cannot be saved, be they never so diligent to frame their lives according to the light of nature, or the laws of that religion which they profess; neither is there salvation in any other, but in Christ alone, who is the Savior only of his body the church.

Not only did seventeenth-century Arminians believe that people could be saved without explicit faith in Christ, David Dickson asserts that the doctrine of the Confession also counters that of the Socinians, who maintained "that men living according to the law and light of nature may be saved."[26] This points us to an important fact: the Confession must be understood as a polemical document. Though it is not elenctic in that it is not a series of affirmations and denials, still it functions both ways. It promotes some doctrines and it opposes others. We need to keep this in mind as we work our way through it.

This expression counters the doctrine of religious sincerity and of the virtuous heathen. According to the Confession, there is no salvation apart from explicit faith in Christ. We encounter this doctrine many times later in the Confession: 2:3, 7:3, 10:4, 20:1-4. We might say that the Baptist positions may be summarized in two ways. While both groups believed in salvation by Christ, the General Baptists acknowledged that people may receive that salvation via either general or special revelation, while the Particular Baptists argued that salvation would only come by means of special revelation. For the General Baptists, Christ's atonement removed the stain of original sin and set man's will free

---

[26] David Dickson, *Truth's Victory over Error* (Edinburgh: The Banner of Truth, 2007, reprint), 1.

to follow whatever light he received. So long as he followed that light, God in Christ would provide him with salvation. For the Particulars, the doctrine of total depravity precluded any sincere acts by fallen men. No one could come to Christ apart from hearing the explicit message of Christ as revealed in Holy Scripture. And so, it demonstrates the necessity of Special revelation.

3. The reality and importance of supernatural revelation

> *Therefore it pleased the Lord at sundry times, and in divers manners, to reveal Himself, and to declare that His will unto His Church . . .*

The Confession at this point recognizes two kinds of special revelation: non-written and inscripturated. It comes progressively in stages: first, there is general revelation, available to all, but this is utterly insufficient to bring men into a saving relationship with God. Then there was personal revelation, given *at sundry times and in divers manners,* but subject to distortion; and so God gave a written revelation for the good of his people. Warfield points out that this addresses two different questions. The first is, was it necessary for God to place special revelation in written form? And the answer is no, he could have chosen to continue the pre-inscripturation process of revelation. It was certainly true and sufficient for men prior to receiving the Scriptures.

4. The complete commitment to inspired Scriptures

> *. . . and afterward for the better preserving, and propagating of the Truth, and for the more sure Establishment, and Comfort of the Church against the corruption of the flesh, and the malice of Satan, and of the World, to commit the same wholly unto writing which maketh the Holy Scriptures to be most necessary, those former ways of Gods revealing his will unto his people being now ceased.*

Warfield's second question is this, is it necessary *now* to believe the Scriptures as the only revelation of God's will to bring men to salvation?[27] And the answer is yes—the former ways of revealing himself have ceased.

5. The consequent necessity of Scripture

Therefore, God's will for man's salvation has been *wholly committed to writing*. It does not rely, in any way as previously, on any method but that of inscripturation. This does not negate the importance and/or continuing validity of general revelation. It simply asserts that it must be viewed in its own sphere. It cannot and will not save anyone. Is it useful? Certainly. God teaches us much through general revelation—we can treat all of the wealth of human knowledge as aspects of general revelation. Why is it bad for your children to eat lead paint chips? What benefits do we receive from scientific inquiry? All of these things fit into the scope of general revelation. But none of them can save us or bring us into a genuine relationship with God. For that, we need the Scriptures.

Nor does this mean that the Scriptures only address matters of salvation, and cannot be trusted in matters of history, science or general knowledge. That misunderstands and misrepresents our doctrine. It is rather that the Scriptures have, *as their primary purpose*, the communication of saving knowledge to men.

What are the implications of the necessity of Scripture? As Dickson points out, this refutes both the Roman Catholic doctrine of the church as infallible, the only interpreter of Scripture in the light of its tradition, as well as the Quaker doctrine of the light of the Spirit apart from the written word.[28] The Scriptures are the foundation left by the apostles, and provide us with a perfect rule by which to order our lives. Since then, general revelation is insufficient, and God's former ways of revealing himself have ceased; Scripture is necessary. Beyond this fact, we should also notice that this is a careful claim to the end of any other modes of special revelation. David Dickson states that 'Enthusiasts and Quakers err' when they 'maintain that the Lord hath not ceased yet

[27] Warfield, *Westminster* Assembly, 195.

[28] Dickson, *Truth's Victory*, 2.

to reveal his will as he did of old.' At the end of his book, he defines 'enthusiasts': "so called from the Greek word ἐνθυσιαζω, or ἐθυσιασω, in Latin *fanatico,* 'I am inspired', or acted with a prophetical or divine fury."[29]

In 2LCF and WCF, the language at this point is identical. In cases where this occurs (and they are many) we may look to the writings of the broader Puritan movement for insight into the meaning and intention of the text. Our Baptist fathers would have been in complete agreement with their Presbyterian and Congregational brothers on this topic. The best modern work on this is Garnet H. Milne, *The Westminster Confession of Faith and the Cessation of Special Revelation*. He demonstrates that the members of the Westminster Assembly wrote extensively on this topic. They were consistently cessationists in their sermons and books.

Milne argues that when the Westminster Divines addressed this matter, three major passages were used in support of their views: Ephesians 1:17 and 18, Hebrews 1:1-2, and Joel 2:28/Acts 2:17-18.[30] In the first, Ephesians 1:17-18, Paul's prayer includes a reference to God's giving "the spirit of wisdom and revelation in the knowledge of Him." According to the Puritan interpreters, this indicated a distinction between 'mediate' and 'immediate' revelation. Mediate revelation came by means of some external source.[31] A person did not directly and personally receive a revelation, but rather it came through another method—i.e., Scripture. In contrast, immediate revelation came directly and personally to the individual receiving it—e.g., dreams, visions, theophanies, etc. The question in Ephesians 1:17-18 is this: does Paul pray for mediate or immediate revelation? Thomas Goodwin, in commenting on this verse, states

---

[29] Dickson, *Truth's Victory*, 3, 269. Please note that the Greek text in this edition of Dickson does not contain diacritical marks.

[30] Garnet H. Milne, *The Westminster Confession of Faith and the Cessation of Special Revelation* (Carlisle: Paternoster, 2007), 109-45.

[31] Benjamin Keach addresses this when speaking of the difference between apostolic preaching and that of his own day, "But certain it is, they preached by an Immediate and extraordinary Spirit or Inspiration; And so do not we, but by an ordinary Spirit from the mediate Word, . . ." Benjamin Keach, *The Breach Repair'd in God's Worship* (London: John Hancock, 1691), 179.

that Paul must mean mediate revelation. Why? Because the text was addressed to *all* of the Ephesian Christians. Throughout Scripture history, immediate revelation was given to certain individuals—even in New Testament times. But here, all are expected to know these things. Goodwin also points to 2 Corinthians 5:16.

The basis for this is the Reformed view that Scripture is final. Samuel Rutherford, in commenting on this text, says that this revelation is "made of things in Scripture."[32] Matthew Henry's commentary remarks:

> We have the revelation of the Spirit in the word: but will that avail us, if we have not the wisdom of the Spirit in the heart? If the same Spirit who indited[33] the sacred scriptures do not take the veil from off our hearts, and enable us to understand and improve them, we shall be never the better.[34]

The idea is that the Spirit always works *with* the Word.

The second text Milne indicates as an important source is Hebrews 1:1-2. In this text, there is a contrast between former methods of revelation and what God has done in his Son. In the past, God used *immediate* revelation. This was a common and frequent means in the ages before. But a final revelation has been made in his Son. The Greek is even more direct.[35] It emphasizes the finality of Christ's revelation as well as the important relationship between Christ and revelation. All revelation must be understood in its relation to Christ as prophet, and Christ the mediator, who

---

32 Samuel Rutherford, *A Survey of the Spirituall Antichrist* (London: Andrew Crooke, 1648) 40. On the title page, the author's surname is spelled "Rutherfurd."Cited in Milne, *Cessation*, 118.

33 'Indited' means to superintended writing (note the linguistic relation to the term edit) and 'improve them' means to live according to their precepts.

34 Matthew Henry, *Matthew Henry's Commentary on the Whole Bible* (Peabody: Hendrickson, 1991 reprint), 6:555. The comments on Ephesians in *Matthew Henry's Commentary* were apparently written by Samuel Rosewell, an associate of and successor to John Howe.

35 The Greek text is Πολυμερῶς καὶ Πολυτρόπως πάλαι ὁ θεὸς λαλήσας τοῖς πατράσιν ἐν τοῖς προφήταις ἐπ' ἐσχάτου τῶν ἡμερῶν τούτων ἐλάλησὲ ἡμῖν ἐν ὑιῷ. The final phrase, ἐν ὑιῷ, is difficult to render precisely in English. Literally it reads 'in Son,' as he is God's final and perfect revelation.

now sits at God's right hand, directs every revelation. The Spirit does not work apart from Him.

Milne's third text is Joel 2:28-32 and its New Testament citation in Acts 2:17. According to Milne, this is an unexpected text to use to teach cessationism. But the observation is important. According to the expositions, Peter says that ***this*** is what Joel wrote about. His point is that the events of the day of Pentecost fulfill the prophetic words of Joel. Not that Joel spoke of an extended period in which these things continue, but rather that the events of that day brought Joel's words to fulfillment. Edward Reynolds, a Westminster divine, said:

> though there be no prophetical, or extraordinary revelations, by dreams, visions, extasies, or enthusiasms; yet according to the measure of spiritual perspicacie, and diligent observation of the Holy Scriptures, there are still manifold revelations or manifestations of Christ unto the soul, the secret and intimate acquaintance of the Soul with God, . . . are pure Heavenly and constant revelations out of the Word manifested to the souls of the faithful by the Spirit.[36]

These are just the most frequent texts to which our confessional fathers would go. But they help us to see the importance of a Christ-centered view of Scripture and the work of the Spirit. The exalted Christ is mediator to the church and works his will by his Spirit through his complete word. There is no need for extra-scriptural revelations.

The same ideas may be seen in our Baptist fathers. Benjamin Keach, in reply to the argument that a special gift of the Spirit is needed for singing, said:

> We have no more reason to lay aside or neglect Singing the Praises of God, till those extraordinary Gifts shall return, (which we have no ground to expect ever will) than we have to lay aside Prayer,

---

[36] Cited in Milne, *Cessation*, 139 from Reynolds treatise *An Explication of Psalm CX*, 48.

> Preaching, Baptism, the Lord's Supper, and every other Duty and Ordinance . . .[37]

And in his *Exposition of the Parables Series* Keach writes:

> Expect no new revelation from God, for God hath established his word forever, he will not alter the thing that is gone out of his mouth; heaven and earth shall pass away, before one jot or tittle of God's word shall pass away. Expect no new revelation, nor any other prophet to be raised up, to discover the mind of God to you, or to make void any thing that is not written, or to teach you otherwise to believe, act, or do, that you may be saved.[38]

Very clearly, the orthodox theologians of the era rejected all forms of 'enthusiasm'—every claim to subsequent revelation beyond the inscripturated word.

Conclusion

The first paragraph of 2LCF is an important doorway into the theology of the following chapters of the document. It sets out a sufficient, infallible, and inerrant basis for building an informed faith. God has given a permanent inscripturated revelation and there is no need for any further divine disclosure. In the following paragraphs, this revelation is clearly defined as the sixty-six books of the Old and New Testaments, which is today called the Bible. It is given by divine inspiration, is authoritative, perfect, and perspicuous. It has been kept through the ages by divine preservation, is self-interpreting, and is the final court of appeal in all doctrinal and practical matters of faith. For these reasons, churches and Christians must look to their Bibles as *"the only sufficient, certain, and infallible rule of all saving Knowledge, Faith and Obedience."*

---

37 Keach, *The Breach Repair'd*, 147.
38 Keach, *Exposition of the Parables Series*, 847.

"DOLPHINS IN THE WOODS":
A Critique of Mark Jones and Ted Van Raalte's Presentation of Particular Baptist Covenant Theology

Samuel Renihan*

No one ever loses a debate. Both sides walk away in victory because they stated their cases correctly. The opponent, of course, completely misunderstood and simply didn't get it. Even the audience agrees. "Our side won." Sadly, most debates are like this, and debates between paedobaptists and Baptists throughout the years have been no exception to the trend. For many centuries the baptismal debate has divided, disappointingly but necessarily, brothers who otherwise share a great deal in common.

In Joel Beeke and Mark Jones' massive and delightful *A Puritan Theology* they have dedicated a chapter to describing this debate as it took place in the late seventeenth century.[1] Their chapter sets out to do two main things: *first,* to vindicate John Owen's covenant theology from Baptist appropriation, and *second,* to demonstrate how John Flavel bested Philip Cary in their printed debate on the subject of covenant theology. This present article will evaluate the portrayal of the Particular Baptists as it is found in that chapter, clarifying how and why the Particular Baptists appropriated John Owen's covenant theology and demonstrating that while the Cary/Flavel debate is useful for illustration, Cary's views must be placed within the context of Particular Baptist federalism as a whole—particularly regarding the conditionality of the covenant of grace and the purpose and design of the Mosaic covenant. This

* Samuel Renihan, M.Div., is a pastor at Trinity Reformed Baptist Church in La Mirada, CA and a Ph.D. student at the Free University of Amsterdam.

[1] The acknowledgments in the introduction state that Ted Van Raalte co-wrote this chapter with Mark Jones. Joel R. Beeke and Mark Jones, *A Puritan Theology: Doctrine for Life* (Grand Rapids, MI: Reformation Heritage Books, 2012), xiv. The chapter referenced is chapter 45 on pages 725-41.

evaluation is not intended to revive the debate itself, but rather to present a fairer and more complete portrait of Particular Baptist federalism and their arguments against paedobaptism.

Abraham, not Moses?

In what ways did the Particular Baptists appeal to John Owen's covenant theology as a support for their own principles? Jones and Van Raalte offer a sparse answer to this question. All that is set forward is that the Particular Baptists agreed with Owen's view that the new covenant differed in substance from the old, as he had argued in his commentary on Hebrews 8.[2] Nehemiah Coxe is given as an example of this agreement, which is of course true.[3] However, other than saying that the Baptists agreed with Owen on this point, and their subsequent emphasis on the newness of the new covenant, nothing else is said. This is an insufficient and incomplete representation of the Baptists' appropriation of Owen, and, being a straw man, is quickly knocked over in his defense.

To vindicate Owen, the argument is asserted that Owen's justification for paedobaptism came from the Abrahamic covenant, not the Mosaic covenant. Thus any appeal to his minority view on the Mosaic covenant does not help one's defense of credobaptism.[4] The heading within the chapter is "Abraham, not Moses," indicating that the Baptists misunderstood the placement of Owen's (and the vast majority of paedobaptists') justification for infant baptism and thus misdirected their polemical efforts.

Operating under this false assumption of the Particular Baptists' understanding of paedobaptist federalism in general and Owen's in particular, a brief sampling of authors (Stephen Marshall, Thomas Goodwin, and Samuel Petto) are used to show that the practice of paedobaptism was universally argued from Abraham's covenant, not Moses' covenant. They state, "These points serve to clarify the

---

[2] Beeke and Jones, *A Puritan Theology*, 725-26.

[3] Cf. Nehemiah Coxe, *A Discourse of the Covenants that God made with Man before the Law* (London: Printed by J.D., 1681), iv.

[4] A helpful presentation of Owen's covenant theology as a deviation from the "majority view" is found in chapter 18 of *A Puritan Theology*, 293-303.

major hermeneutical issue in the debate. Reformed theologians have always made it clear that the warrant for paedobaptism does not come from Moses."[5] This vindicates Owen because "One may argue that the new covenant is different in kind than the Sinaitic or old covenant . . . but Owen . . . could affirm paedobaptism . . . because all agreed that the command to baptize infants was based on the perpetual promise made to Abraham."[6]

A concluding acknowledgement states that "the more learned antipaedobaptists" were aware of the fact that the justification of infant baptism came from Abraham, not Moses. Whether this statement is directed at modern or ancient Baptists is unclear.[7] Wherever the statement is directed, it is misleading. Particular Baptists, in 1644 or 2015, have not failed to locate the exegetical argument of paedobaptism.[8]

To reshape and properly portray the Particular Baptists' side of these assertions, we need to start at the beginning. It is important to remember that the first generation of Particular Baptists were originally paedobaptists themselves.[9] They were not continental Anabaptists; they were English separatists who moved from a standard paedobaptist position to a Baptist position, and they did not do so lightly.[10] On that basis alone it should not be surprising

---

[5] Beeke and Jones, *A Puritan Theology*, 728.

[6] Beeke and Jones, *A Puritan Theology*, 728.

[7] A footnote references Mike Renihan's dissertation on the Anglican antipaedobaptist John Tombes. If the antipaedobaptists who understood the argument for infant baptism from the Abrahamic covenant were "more learned," then we can say they were all "more learned" because they all understood it quite well.

[8] This point should be obvious from the second half of Jones and Van Raalte's chapter which deals with Cary and Flavel's debate concerning the interpretation of the Abrahamic covenant.

[9] On the genesis and development of the Particular Baptists see James M. Renihan *Edification and Beauty: The Practical Ecclesiology of the English Particular Baptists, 1675-1705* (Milton Keynes, UK: Paternoster, 2008), 1-36. Cf. also Michael A. G. Haykin, *Kiffin, Knollys, and Keach* (Leeds: Reformation Today, 1996), 15-32.

[10] On the one hand, they suffered a great deal of persecution at the hands of the various authorities, whether Anglican or Presbyterian (or Congregational in America). It would be more difficult to name a Particular Baptist minister who *wasn't* put in jail at some point, than to name one that was. On the other hand, they

that the Particular Baptists were well versed in the justification of paedobaptism. Additionally, they read the writings of the Reformers, the early orthodox, their contemporaries, and they were engaged in printed and formal debates from the very inception of their further reformation of the church. They did not live in isolation.

From those earliest days, they aimed their sights at the Abrahamic covenant. In 1645, Benjamin Coxe, William Kiffin, and Hanserd Knollys had made plans with Edmund Calamy to debate this issue. The debate never took place, due to a variety of circumstances, however the three men mentioned above published a list of the arguments which they would have used against Calamy and infant baptism. One of those arguments was:

> We conceive, that this Scripture [Gal. 3:29; Rom. 9:6-9] doth expound, Gen. 17. God made an everlasting covenant of Grace with ABRAHAM and his seed. Now the Scriptures declare, that ABRAHAM had two kindes of seed; one born after the flesh, the other born after the Spirit, Gal. 4. 29. The question is, who are counted for *Abrahams* seed according to the covenant of grace?[11]

They go on to connect this twofold seed to *two different covenants.* Using Galatians 4 to interpret Genesis 17, they argue as follows:

---

consulted eminent paedobaptist theologians in their journey from paedobaptism. For example, Henry Jessey consulted theologians as eminent as "Mr Nye, Mr Tho Goodwin, Mr Burroughs, Mr Greenhill, Mr Cradock, Mr Carter, & with Mr Jackson, Mr Bolton, &c." Benjamin Stinton, *A Repository of Divers Historical Matters relating to the English Antipedobaptists Collected from Original Papers of Faithful Extracts* (Unpublished manuscript, 1712), 28.

11 Benjamin Coxe, William Kiffin, and Hanserd Knollys, *A Declaration Concerning the Publike Dispute Which Should have been in the Publike Meeting-House of Alderman-Bury, the 3d of this instant Moneth of December; Concerning Infants-Baptisme. Together, with some of the Arguments which should have been propounded and urged by some of those that are falsly called Anabaptists, which should then have disputed* (London: n.p., 1645), 16. Italics original. One of the reasons why the debate never took place was that a report was made to the authorities that the Particular Baptists planned to bring weapons and kill Calamy.

> The Apostle witnesseth, that these are two Covenants, which GOD made with ABRAHAM and his seed; to wit, a covenant of Workes with *Abrahams* fleshly seed, and a covenant of Grace with *Abrahams* spirituall seed. . . . And here hath Mr. *Cal.* and his brethren been mistaken, in bringing an Argument to prove Infant baptisme, drawn from *Abrahams* fleshly seed; affirming, that there is but one Covenant in that Scripture, and that is a covenant of Grace.[12]

This example serves to illustrate two things. First, it illustrates that from their beginning, the Particular Baptists specifically disagreed with the justification of paedobaptism as it was argued from Genesis 17 and the Abrahamic covenant. Second, it illustrates a common hermeneutical move in which the Particular Baptists saw *two* covenants in Genesis 17, the covenant of circumcision (a covenant of works to the fleshly seed of Abraham), and the covenant of grace delivered in promise form to the elect. They would then draw a line from circumcision to the Mosaic covenant, connecting Abraham and Moses on the level of the Israelite nation. Space does not permit examples to be given to trace this argumentation through the Particular Baptists,[13] but the present

---

[12] Coxe, Kiffin, and Knollys, *A Declaration*, 16-17. Italics original. Jones and van Raalte draw attention to Marshall's (and others') accusation that the doctrine that children do not belong to the covenant of grace by birth "puts all the Infants of all Believers into the self-same condition with the Infants of Turks, and Indians." Beeke and Jones, *A Puritan Theology*, 728. Coxe, Kiffin, and Knollys responded by saying, "But some may think, that this will put the children of Believers into as bad a condition, as the children of Turkes, Heathens, and any other wicked men; and this they are perswaded is a horrible thing, and a dangerous opinion. We put not the children of Believers into as bad a condition as the children of Turkes, &c. It was *Adams* disobedience in eating the forbidden fruit, that put all his posterity equally into a sinfull and miserable condition, Rom. 5. 12. 19. And the doctrine which Mr. CAL. and his brethren teach, doth the like. They say (and it is truth) that all the Infants of Believers...are born in sin, and are by nature children of wrath as well as others. And now let the Reader judge, Whether this their own doctrine, do not put the children of Believers into as bad a condition." Coxe, Kiffin, and Knollys, *A Declaration*, 17.

[13] See Thomas Patient's seven arguments to prove circumcision to be a covenant of works. Thomas Patient, *The Doctrine of Baptism and the Distinction of the Covenants* (London: Printed by Henry Hills, 1654), 44-71. Cf. also Christopher

point is that Particular Baptist federalism was not so simplistic as to think that the Mosaic covenant being a covenant of works would end the entire debate. They did not miss the point, nor did they fail to locate and wrestle with the exegetical ground of infant baptism.

Abraham, and Moses

Having given a more appropriate view of the background and nature of Particular Baptist covenant theology, and having set down a very basic form of their federalism and covenantal polemic against infant baptism, it should come as no surprise that even in their use of Owen the Particular Baptists did not look only to his views on the Mosaic covenant. Before Owen's volume on Hebrews 6-10 was published, the Particular Baptists argued that his views on the Abrahamic covenant itself lined up with their own. Edward Hutchinson and Thomas Delaune are examples of this.

In 1676, Edward Hutchinson wrote *A Treatise Concerning the Covenant and Baptism* in which he continued the standard Particular Baptist method of making twofold distinctions in God's federal dealings with Abraham. Abraham had two seeds, one natural and the other spiritual. And these two seeds represent the membership of two different covenants. The covenant of grace was comprised of the elect and ran through Christ himself. The covenant of circumcision, or the covenant of peculiarity, was comprised of Abraham's physical children and ran through Abraham as a human father.[14] To whom does Hutchinson appeal on this point? He

---

Blackwood, *The Storming of Antichrist, In his two last and strongest Garrisons; of Compulsion of Conscience, and Infants Babptisme* (London: n.p., 1644), 31, 35; Blackwood, *Apostolicall Baptisme, Or A Sober Rejoynder to a Book written by Mr. Thomas Blake* (n.p., 1646), 57-60; Coxe, *A Discourse of the Covenants*, 67-195.

14 Edward Hutchinson, *A Treatise Concerning the Covenant and Baptism Dialogue-wise, between a Baptist & a Poedo-Baptist* (London: Printed for Francis Smith, 1676), 27. See also pg. 93, 95 where he calls the Abrahamic covenant a covenant of works and a political covenant.

appeals to the first volume of Owen's commentary on the book of Hebrews, and quotes a lengthy portion of it to his own advantage.[15]

The initial points made by Owen are summarized as follows:

1. God gave a twofold privilege to Abraham:
    a. The messiah would be born from his line, making his descendants a special people. This privilege was to end when Christ was born.
    b. Abraham's faith would be the pattern for the church in all ages, and only those who believe as he did are his spiritual children.
2. This resulted in a twofold seed:
    a. A seed according to the flesh, separated for the bringing forth of the Messiah.
    b. A seed according to the promise, i.e. those that have faith in the promise, or all the elect of God.[16]

Owen applies these truths by saying:

> Now it is evident, that it is the *second Priviledge* and spiritual seed, wherein the Church to whom the Promises are made is founded, and whereof it doth consist, namely in them, who by faith are interested in the Covenant of *Abraham*, whether they be of the carnal seed or no.[17]

The argument is continued by Owen to show how the Jews were greatly mistaken in thinking that their lineage could entitle them to the promises of the covenant of grace. And he concludes, "The church unto whom all the *Promises* belong, are only those who are Heirs of *Abrahams* Faith; believing as he did, and thereby interested in his Covenant."[18]

---

[15] He quotes John Owen, *Exercitations on the Epistle to the Hebrews...With an Exposition and Discourses on the Two First Chapters of the said Epistle to the Hebrews* (London: Printed by Robert White, 1668), 55-56, 57.

[16] Owen, *Exercitations on the Epistle to the Hebrews*, 55. Owen points out that these two seeds intermingled. Ishmael was a child according to the flesh, not the promise. Isaac was both.

[17] Owen, *Exercitations on the Epistle to the Hebrews*, 55. Italics original.

[18] Owen, *Exercitations on the Epistle to the Hebrews*, 56 Italics original.

Hutchinson considered this to be ample evidence to justify the credobaptist principle that "*Believers only are the children of Abraham, and none but such have an Interest in the Covenant made with him,* which unavoidably excludes infants from Gospel-Ordinances, until they believe in their own persons."[19] Knowing, of course, that Owen was not a credobaptist, Hutchinson added:

> And if our opponents think Dr. O. injured (as they are apt to clamour to that purpose) for our improvement of his words to our advantage . . . we say, that they are at liberty to reconcile his words to his practice if they can, to do which they have need of a considerable stock (but they are seldome unfurnisht) of artifice, and distinction, to help at this dead lift.[20]

Hutchinson was well aware of what he was doing. And he knew that the paedobaptists would not appreciate it.

One such paedobaptist was Joseph Whiston, who wrote against Hutchinson that same year. Whiston said, "I should be justly censured as a very unworthy Man, should I wrest Authors words . . . to countenance my own sentiments in a contradiction to their known practice."[21] He adds:

> He [Owen] meddles not with the case of Infants, but supposeth them visibly in Covenant as the Seed of Parents visibly so; when will you leave thus to abuse Authors whose names are so precious in all the Churches of Christ?[22]

Whiston's appeal to visible membership in the covenant serves to highlight the two main fronts on which the Particular Baptists launched their critique of paedobaptism: covenant theology and positive law. Concerning covenant theology, the Particular Baptists argued that only the members of the covenant should receive the covenant sign, and since children were not members by birth they

---

19 Hutchinson, *A Treatise Concerning the Covenant*, 34. Italics original.

20 Hutchinson, *A Treatise Concerning the Covenant*, 34-35.

21 Joseph Whiston, *An Essay to Revive the Primitive Doctrine and Practice of Infant-Baptism* (London: Printed for Jonathan Robinson, 1676), 253.

22 Whiston, *An Essay to Revive the Primitive Doctrine*, 253.

should not receive the sign. Complementary to this initial argument was the case from positive law. The Particular Baptists argued that even if the premise were granted that children are included in the covenant, baptism could only be administered according to its positive institution, which required a profession of faith. It was the same, they argued, in circumcision and all ordinances. Circumcision was for males only, and only on the 8th day. It was not simply administered to all members of the covenant. So even if infants were included in the covenant, there was still no command to administer baptism to them.[23]

Hutchinson's citation of Owen played into the Particular Baptists' hands on the first front, excluding infants from the covenant, in their opinion, because infants are not the children of Abraham by faith. Whiston defended Owen based on the fact that visibly speaking, the administration was to be given to children.[24]

Thomas Delaune responded to Whiston the following year, saying:

> What the *Doctor* supposes to *Infants being in the Covenant, in his Judgement or practice* concerns not the matter in hand. . . . And, I am as certain, that the *Doctors* discourse of the Covenant, wholly excludes them from any such title. And if Mr. *Whiston* can no

---

[23] For an example of this, see Hutchinson, *A Treatise Concerning the Covenant*, 58. Cf. also Henry Danvers, *A Treatise of Baptism: Wherein That of Believers and that of Infants is examined by the Scriptures* (London: Printed for Francis Smith, 1673), 205-06. Cf. Coxe, *A Discourse of the Covenants*, 131.

[24] Whiston is using the classic paedobaptist distinction between external/internal membership of the covenant. This is an important tangent that we cannot follow at the present. But the question was often asked by Particular Baptists as to what it means to be in the covenant "visibly" or "externally." If the paedobaptists admitted that their infants were not automatically of the substance of the covenant (to make such a claim is to say they are elect), but rather participated only in the administration (the external ordinances) then do they not remain in the covenant of works, under Adam's federal headship? And if that is the case, in what sense are they in the covenant of grace? This was hinted at in footnote 12 above. Samuel Richardson said, "No interest in Christ, no interest in the Covenant and promises thereof." Samuel Richardson, *Some Brief Considerations on Doctor Featley his Book, intituled, The Dipper Dipt* (London: n.p., 1645), 12.

> better reconcile the *Doctors* words to his *Practice*, he had better have held his peace.[25]

This back-and-forth is not surprising. Whiston did not feel the need to resolve Owen's assertions, knowing that Owen still maintained infant baptism. And the Particular Baptists saw this as a contradiction but were content to leave the resolution to their paedobaptist brothers.

What must be recognized is that the Particular Baptists used Owen's views on the Abrahamic covenant *and* the Mosaic covenant to support their credobaptist principles and practices. Yet even so, they did not leave the argument to a simple appeal to Owen.

Nehemiah Coxe, put forward in *A Puritan Theology* as the example of Particular Baptists misguidedly assuming that Owen's views championed their own, is a perfect illustration of this fact. In his preface, Coxe directed the reader to Owen's views on the Mosaic covenant yet then proceeded to dedicate no less than four chapters spanning 128 pages to God's covenantal dealings with Abraham, including a chapter entitled "Of the Mutual Respect of the Promises made to Abraham."

In that chapter he said:

> The *typical Respect and Analogy of the Covenant of Peculiarity unto the Covenant of Grace*, as after to be more fully revealed, and accomplished in Christ, affords another Occasion of, and Reason for, the *interweaving* of those Promises which require a distinct Application: some of them belonging immediately to the carnal, and others to the spiritual Seed, as arising from the springs, and ordered towards the Ministration of two distinct Covenants.[26]

Coxe was aware that on the one hand they had a strong ally in Owen on the Mosaic covenant, and on the other hand they needed to address the Abrahamic covenant specifically.

---

[25] Thomas Delaune, *Truth Defended: Or, A Triple Answer to the late Triumvirates Opposition in their Three Pamphlets, Viz. Mr. Baxter's Review, Mr. Wills his Censure, Mr. Whiston's Postscript to his Essay, &c.* (London: Printed for the author, 1677), 20. Italics original.

[26] Coxe, *A Discourse of the Covenants*, 169. Italics original.

More than anything, it was Owen's hermeneutical sensitivity to the dual nature of God's dealings with Abraham and the nation of Israel that drew such vocal Particular Baptist support. This was significant because the argument that the old and new covenants were *one* in substance was used over and over again in order to assert that it was only the administration, or outward ordinances, that had changed.[27] Circumcision replaced baptism, etc. The champions of this majority view were not unaware of the duality of God's dealings with Abraham or the nation of Israel, they simply treated them as external quantitative or accidental differences. But in the case of the Mosaic covenant, Owen was willing to see far more than a change of outward ordinances. He was willing to see *two different covenants.* This was a strong and welcome push from an unexpected and much-appreciated ally.[28]

---

[27] David Dickson likened the difference between the administrations to a man dressing one way in his youth, and another in his adult years. It was purely an outward difference, one thing in two different forms. David Dickson, *Therapeutica Sacra* (Edinburgh, Printed by Evan Tyler, 1664), 98; also *Truths Victory over Error* (Edinburgh: Printed by John Reed, 1684), 50-55.

[28] The significance of Owen's departure from the majority should not be missed. His departure was significant because his view *contradicts* and is *incompatible* with the majority view as laid down in the Westminster Confession. In a way, this is obvious. Owen himself lays out the majority view, and *rejects* it. Owen, *A Continuation of the Exposition of the Epistle of Paul the Apostle to the Hebrews* (London: Printed for Nathaniel Ponder, 1680), 224-42. This is also evident from the writings of John Ball, one of the well-known sources for the Westminster Confession's covenant theology. See Andrew Woolsey, *Unity and Continuity in Covenantal Thought* (Grand Rapids, MI: Reformation Heritage Books, 2012), 45-79. As Ball dealt with three different ways to handle the Mosaic covenant he described John Cameron's view, though not naming him. John Ball, *A Treatise of the Covenant of Grace* (London: Printed by G. Miller, 1645), 93-95. Ball follows Cameron's arguments exactly. Cf. John Cameron, *Certain Theses, or, Positions of the Learned John Cameron, Concerning the three-fold Covenant of God with Man* in Samuel Bolton, *The True Bounds of Christian Freedome* (London: Printed by J.L., 1645), 382-95. Having described this view, Ball concludes, "By this explication it appears, the Divines of this opinion, make the old Covenant differ from the new in substance, and kind, and not in degree of manifestation." Owen's position on the Mosaic covenant is the same as Cameron's in the sense that both see it as neither the covenant of works, nor the covenant of grace, but a distinct legal covenant for the nation of Israel to live life in the land. Both Ball and Owen agree that his view is out of bounds for a

The Particular Baptists essentially applied the same hermeneutic to the Abrahamic covenant as Owen had (and they before him) to the Mosaic covenant. The dual referents in the Abrahamic covenant related to *distinct covenants*. Within a Particular Baptist framework, the line from Abrahamic circumcision to being bound to the full extent of the laws of the Mosaic covenant was an exegetical and direct path to follow. Thus, if Owen ceded that the Mosaic covenant was *not* the covenant of grace but was a covenant of works for the natural descendants of Abraham, and if he ceded that Abraham's twofold seed can be reduced to believers and Abraham's natural children, while also ceding that the rights of the natural offspring ended at the institution of the new covenant, the Particular Baptists had gained some valuable steps forward in Owen.[29]

There is no doubt that Owen continued to justify infant baptism from the Abrahamic covenant, in spite of these things. In the same

"one covenant, two administrations" view as expressed in the Westminster Confession of Faith.

29 There is a great deal more that could be said about how Owen's views in his commentary on Hebrews 6-10 played into Particular Baptist hands. For example, Owen's treatment of the Abrahamic covenant in Hebrews 6 closely follows his views already mentioned in the first volume of his Hebrews commentary. See Owen, *A Continuation of the Exposition*, 135-47. Later in his commentary, Owen described the Abrahamic covenant, in contrast to the new covenant, as being made "with respect unto other things, especially the proceeding of the promised Seed from his loins." Owen, *A Continuation of the Exposition*, 227. Considering Owen's distinctions above, he is referring to the fact that the Abrahamic covenant was primarily about his natural descendants being set apart as a special people in order to bring about the birth of the Messiah. It was not the actual establishment of the new covenant in Christ's blood, nor the actual source of the salvation of the elect. This also played into Particular Baptist hands because Owen argued that in the Old Testament the new covenant existed in promise form only, not having its own worship and ordinances yet. The covenant of grace considered absolutely in promise form was the source of salvation for the elect in the Old Testament, but it was not a formal covenant until Christ shed his blood. The Particular Baptists took this one step further (well before Owen) and called the Abrahamic covenant a distinct covenant, the covenant of circumcision or the covenant of peculiarity. Owen did everything but that, and through his views on the Mosaic covenant the pieces were in place for such a move, according to the Particular Baptists. Owen, *A Continuation of the Exposition*, 227.

commentary, while considering the meaning of Hebrews 6:2, Owen wrote:

> There were two sorts of persons that were baptized, namely, those that were *adult* at their first hearing of the Gospel, and the *infant Children of Believers* who were admitted to be members of the Church . . . being received as a *part and branches* of a Family whereupon the blessing of *Abraham* was come, and to whom the *Promises of the Covenant* was extended.[30]

In conclusion of this section, wherever Owen's views logically lead, the Particular Baptists used his insights not simply on the Mosaic covenant, but also the Abrahamic covenant. In light of this, *A Puritan Theology*'s representation of Owen's justification of infant baptism may be accurate, but its presentation of the Particular Baptists' appropriation of Owen and understanding of paedobaptist polemics is not. The Particular Baptists did not miss the location of the justification of infant baptism, nor did they appeal to Owen only on the Mosaic covenant. Thus, pointing out the common use of the Abrahamic covenant as the justification for infant baptism as a reply to the Particular Baptist appropriation of Owen does nothing but make a false implication that the Particular Baptists would not have understood this. As Edward Hutchinson said, quoted above, "And if our opponents think Dr. O. injured (as they are apt to clamour to that purpose) for our improvement of his words to our advantage . . . we say, that they are at liberty to reconcile his words to his practice if they can."

Carrying on the Debate

The second and larger section of Jones and Van Raalte's chapter is dedicated to following the written debate between Philip Cary and John Flavel. My present concern is not to dispute the presentation of that debate, which contains enough quotations from each side to

---

[30] Owen, *A Continuation of the Exposition*, 32. Italics original. On the following page, Owen uses Mark 10:16 to show that Jesus "Owned *little Children* to belong to his Covenant." Italics original.

offer a sufficient idea of their respective affirmations and denials in dialogue. My concern, as in the first half of this article, is to broaden the horizon and offer a more balanced presentation of the Particular Baptists as a whole.

In a footnote, Jones and Van Raalte state that Philip Cary serves as an illustrative character of the Particular Baptists because his covenant theology will be seen to be in line with, they say, Nehemiah Coxe, Richard Allen, John Tombes, and Benjamin Keach.[31] The implication is that Cary's views are representative of the whole of the Particular Baptists.

In ways, this implication is true. For example, as laid out above, it was a majority and standard argument among Particular Baptists that the Mosaic covenant *and* the Abrahamic covenant were covenants of works. On this foundational level there is a great deal of continuity between Cary, his Baptist brothers in general, and the men who signed the preface to his book, *A Solemn Call*. More specifically, as Jones and Van Raalte note, Cary's argument that the Adamic, Abrahamic, and Mosaic covenants were "editions" of the covenant of works is very similar to Benjamin Keach's argument that these three covenants were three "administrations" of the covenant of works.[32]

But in other ways, this implication is untrue. The Particular Baptists' views on the conditionality of the covenant of grace and the purpose and design of the Mosaic covenant need to be

---

[31] Beeke and Jones, *A Puritan Theology*, 729, n. 29. Richard Allen was a General Baptist. John Tombes was an Anglican antipaedobaptist.

[32] See Philip Cary, *A Solemn Call Unto all that would be owned as Christ's Faithful Witnesses, speedily, and seriously, to attend unto the Primitive Purity of the Gospel Doctrine and Worship: Or, a Discourse concerning Baptism* (London: Printed for John Harris, 1690), 119-87. See also, Benjamin Keach, *The Everlasting Covenant, A Sweet Cordial for a Drooping Soul: Or, The Excellent Nature of the Covenant of Grace Opened* (London: Printed for H. Barnard, 1692), 7-8. It is interesting to note that John Bunyan, whose preaching receives an entire chapter in *A Puritan Theology*, held that the Mosaic covenant was *the* covenant of works. For his view see John Bunyan, *The Doctrine of the Lavv and Grace Unfolded: Or, A Discourse touching the Law and Grace* (London: Printed for M. Wright, 1659), 4-19. If you've ever wondered why Adam and Moses act towards Christian in the way that they do in *Pilgrim's Progress*, this is why. They stand for the covenant of works, not just the law.

examined carefully. By extrapolating Cary's views on these two positions to the Particular Baptists, Jones and Van Raalte draw a very unnecessary and unsound conclusion, that "Their position is one step closer to what would later be affirmed in dispensationalist circles—that the Old Testament saints were saved in a different way from the New Testament saints."[33] I will address the ways in which Cary's positions are or are not representative of the whole, and why the conclusion regarding dispensationalism is seriously misguided.

The Conditionality of the Covenant of Grace

While reading Cary and Flavel's debate as presented in *A Puritan Theology*, it becomes clear that conditionality was at the heart of the debate. Cary's insistence on the freedom of the benefits of the covenant of grace led him to the point of denying any conditionality, at least initially. And Flavel, focusing in on this extreme by Cary, used it as the recurring point of argumentation on nearly every issue. As Jones and Van Raalte point out, Cary clarified—or modified—his position to say that faith was a "necessary means in order to receiving" forgiveness of sins.[34] This concession should be enough to demonstrate that the debate

---

[33] Beeke and Jones, *A Puritan Theology*, 740. This is quite the anachronism. If such views indicate movement "one step closer to dispensationalism," it is one step closer on a pathway of 1,000 steps. Lest we forget, the major figures and founders of Dispensationalism in America sprang from Congregationalist (Scofield, who later became a Southern Presbyterian) and Presbyterian (Chafer) backgrounds, not Baptists. Vern Poythress, "Presbyterianism and Dispensationalism" in *The Practical Calvinist: An Introduction to the Presbyterian and Reformed Heritage* (ed. Peter A. Lillback, Ross-Shire, Scotland, UK: Christian Focus Publications, 2002), 415-24. The same argument could be raised in reverse, that by perpetuation of the model of Abraham's family as the paradigm for covenant membership the paedobaptists legitimize the Dispensationalists' expectations of the continuation of Israelite national promises. If Abraham's covenant is our covenant, that is a "step closer" to Dispensationalist Jewish nationalism. This is an unhelpful, fruitless, and groundless avenue of argumentation. See more below.

[34] Philip Cary, *A Just Reply to Mr. John Flavell's Arguments* (London: Printed for J. Harris, 1690), 34.

became quite semantic in some unnecessary ways.[35] Notwithstanding, Cary's dislike for the term "condition" relative to the covenant of grace should not be universally attributed to the Particular Baptists.

There is diversity but general agreement in the way that the Baptists approached the idea of conditionality in the covenant of grace in the seventeenth century. But before entering into their statements it is important to remember that how you approach this issue often determines how you answer it. Herman Witsius has a very helpful discussion of the covenant of grace strictly (or narrowly) considered in which he asserts that from the narrow angle of pure promises there can be no conditions whatsoever in the covenant. Witsius then continues to give a careful and excellent explanation of the sense in which faith is a condition of the covenant of grace.[36] It is the narrow and strict sense of the covenant of grace that most of the Particular Baptists have in mind when they approach this issue, thus they tend toward emphasizing the unconditionality of the covenant of grace. They are usually dealing with Paul's contrast of faith and works in Romans and Galatians, affirming their mutual exclusivity in terms of salvation. However, most also acknowledge the necessity and place of faith as a "condition" for appropriating salvation. A few examples, arranged chronologically, will prove the point.

Thomas Kilcop said, "A condition required thereto is one thing, and a cause thereof is another. . . . Though faith be not a conditional cause of, yet it is so requisite to salvation."[37]

Thomas Patient said:

---

[35] Cf. Obadiah Sedgwick, *The Bowels of Tender Mercy Sealed in the Everlasting Covenant* (London: Edward Mottershed, 1661), 182. "I know there is a great dispute *How any condition can be allowed in a Covenant of Grace*...But I humbly conceive that there is no need of such heat . . . if parties would but patiently hear one another, and calmly consider the matter." Italics original.

[36] Herman Witsius, *The Economy of the Covenants Between God & Man*, vol. 1 (Kingsburg, CA: den Dulk Foundation, 1990), 286-91.

[37] Thomas Kilcop, *Ancient and Durable Gospel* (London: Printed by H.H., 1648), 100.

> It is true, the promise of salvation and remission of Sins, is held out with a condition to the world. . . . But we are not to think, that this grace of Faith and Repentance, are any Qualifications that persons are to attain by their own abilities unto which the Gospel is tendred.[38]

Later he adds, "But in the new covenant, the Lord undertakes to work the condition, and to give the salvation tendred upon that condition."[39]

Daniel King said:

> The Covenant is absolute, free without condition: Nay, the conditions of the promise are absolutely promised in the Covenant: so that they all, promises and conditions both, have their rise from the Covenant. And therefore by virtue of the Covenant we have faith given, which is the condition to salvation.[40]

Robert Purnell, after asserting that the covenant of grace is unconditional in the sense that it does not demand righteousness in us but grants righteousness to us in Christ, answers the following objection, "Some say that this Covenant is conditionall, no otherwise, then in respect of Gods order and method, in bestowing the blessings of it upon us." Purnell replied, "In this sense it may be granted (it is so) still keeping close to this, that not in a proper, but in an improper sense, the Covenant may be said to be conditionall."[41]

Edward Hutchinson referred to the covenant of grace as "the Covenant of Eternal life and salvation, which was made with all the elect in Christ upon the condition of faith."[42]

---

[38] Patient, *The Doctrine of Baptism*, 35.

[39] Patient, *The Doctrine of Baptism*, 35.

[40] Daniel King, *A Way to Sion Sought out and Found* (London: Printed by Christopher Higgins, 1656), 16.

[41] Robert Purnell, *A Little Cabinet Richly Stored with all sorts of Heavenly Varieties, and Soul-reviving Influences* (London: Printed by R. W., 1657), 33-34.

[42] Hutchinson, *A Treatise Concerning the Covenant*, 93.

Benjamin Keach, drawing from Isaac Chauncy, distinguished between "fœderal" conditions (or procuring conditions) and conditions of "connexion." He assigned faith to the latter set of conditions, acknowledging its necessity in terms of sequence and instrumentality but denying any merit or obtaining of blessings thereby.[43]

Lastly, and breaking the chronological order, Nehemiah Coxe provides an instance of careful and knowledgeable distinctions on this point. In his work on the covenants, he acknowledged that covenants are "to be considered, either simply as proposed by God, or as Man enters thereinto by Restipulation."[44] Later, while describing man's restipulation in a covenant, Coxe adds:

> If the Covenant be *of Works*, the Restipulation must be, by *doing* the things required in it, even by fulfilling its condition in *a perfect obedience to the Law of it*. . . . But if it be a Covenant of free and soveraign Grace, the Restipulation required, is *an humble receiving*, or *hearty believing* of those gratuitous Promises on which the Covenant is established.[45]

Coxe understands that covenants involve restipulation, and that different kinds of covenants correlate to different kinds of responses on man's part. Thus, if Coxe were to approach the question from God's monopleuristic proposal of the covenant, it could be called absolute. And if he were to approach the question from the dipleuristic restipulation of the covenant partner, it could be called conditional.

At least one example can be found of a Particular Baptist who explicitly denied faith to be the condition of the covenant of grace.[46]

---

43 Benjamin Keach, *The Display of Glorious Grace: Or, The Covenant of Peace, Opened.* (London: Printed by S. Bridge, 1698), 185-87. Jonathan Arnold provides a helpful discussion of Keach's covenant theology in general, and his views on conditionality in particular in Jonathan W. Arnold, *The Reformed Theology of Benjamin Keach (1640-1704)* (Oxford: Regent's Park College, 2013), 153-56.

44 Coxe, *A Discourse of the Covenants*, 4.

45 Coxe, *A Discourse of the Covenants*, 9. Italics original.

46 Cf. Anon, *Truth Vindicated in Several Branches thereof* (London, Printed for the Author, 1695), 25-27. This anonymous author, presumed to be a Particular Baptist

Samuel Richardson said, "If man had been to performe any of the conditions of this Covenant, it had not been a covenant of grace, but a covenant of works. . . . Nor were the covenant of grace free and absolute, if it were conditionall, for that covenant is not absolute, which depends, upon any condition to be by us performed."[47] Later he adds, "This shews they mistake who conceive the covenant is made with man, or that teach faith to be a condition of the covenant."[48] But he was opposed by his own brothers. Robert Purnell said, "And surely mistaken is Mr. *Samuel Richardson*, that saith...that there is no means to be used by man to get an interest in this Covenant."[49] Richardson's statements took place in the context of a sinner pleading for help in obtaining salvation. So Purnell addressed that same sinner, saying, "1. Break your Covenant with your old sins. . . . 2. Come with an humble submission to...the will of God. . . . 3. Come before God in the name of a Mediator. . . . 4. By faith look at the gracious invitations of God."[50] Despite their differences, both men understood that only God could enable the sinner to perform these actions.

These examples serve to prove that Cary's strongest statements about the unconditionality of the covenant of grace should be read in the larger context of Particular Baptist covenant theology. Within that context, Cary's statements cannot and should not be used to present the Particular Baptists as denying that faith is a necessary prerequisite and "condition" of the covenant of grace. They did

---

based on his arguments, is another instance of asserting the unconditionality of the covenant of grace. He does so because he collapses the covenant of redemption into the new covenant, saying that all has been accomplished for us. He does qualify that God requires duties of his people, but they are not conditions. This seems to represent a more extreme position like that of Samuel Richardson. It should be noted, however, that the author is once again talking in the context of contrasting the promises of the covenant of grace with the demands of the covenant of works.

[47] Samuel Richardson, *Divine Consolations* (London: Printed by M. Simmons, 1649), 224.

[48] Richardson, *Divine Consolations*, 227.

[49] Purnell, *A Little Cabinet*, 43.

[50] Purnell, *A Little Cabinet*, 44. Cf. Samuel Richardson, *The Saints Desire; Or A Cordiall for a fainting soule* (London. Printed by M. Simmons, 1647), 45-48.

confess this in their confession of faith, after all.[51] Nor should his statements be taken to indicate that the Particular Baptists did not understand the single and double aspect of a covenant. Rather, these statements should be taken generally in the context of contrasting the demands of the covenant of works with the promises of the covenant of grace, taken in its narrow sense.

As Jones and Van Raalte conclude their chronicle of Flavel and Cary's debate, they state that Flavel's nuance and precision on this point, and others, place him "well within the broad Reformed tradition."[52] The inference is that Cary's struggle to handle the tension of the conditionality of the covenant of grace, and his apparent tip of the scales towards an extreme, place him *without* the broad Reformed tradition, or at least on its fringes. The examples provided should remedy this inference and offer a more complete perspective of the Particular Baptists.

The Purpose and Design of the Mosaic Covenant

The second point where the Particular Baptists' voices offer more than what has been presented is in the design and purpose of the Mosaic Covenant. This will counteract two claims, first that Cary's views are representative of the Particular Baptists as a whole, and second, that the Particular Baptists opened the door for a theology that posits that Old Testament believers were saved in a different way from that of New Testament believers.

One of the points of debate that gets lost between Cary and Flavel, and in the presentation of *A Puritan Theology*, is that the Particular Baptists' concern was not so much the presence of conditions in the Mosaic covenant in general, but the *kind* of conditions present in the Mosaic covenant. Behind this are at least two controlling factors in covenant theology, Baptist or paedobaptist. One is the use of Galatians 4 and the contrast of the

---

[51] Anon., *A Confession of Faith Put Forth by the Elders and Brethren of Many Congregations of Christians (Baptized Upon Profession of their Faith) in London and the Country* (London: n.p., 1677), 27, (2LCF 7.3).

[52] Beeke and Jones, *A Puritan Theology*, 739.

"two" covenants. The other, closely related, is the use of the idea of the "substance" of a given covenant.

In Galatians 4, Paul describes "the two covenants," which Reformed theology has often identified either as the two dispensations/administrations/testaments of the covenant of grace or as the covenant of works and the covenant of grace.[53] Depending on how a given theologian understood and used this controlling contrast, they interpreted the covenants in Scripture accordingly.

For some, a post-fall covenant of works could easily be found in Moses because Paul contrasted two covenants between Moses and Christ. For others, a post-fall covenant of works was literally impossible because the two-covenant contrast, taken dogmatically, referred to Adam and Christ. The covenant of works could not be remade after the fall. The majority of Reformed theology took the latter option, as expressed in the Westminster Confession of Faith, but by no means was it a uniform view in the seventeenth (or sixteenth) centuries. Nevertheless, common affirmations united all, such as the fall in Adam and salvation by grace alone through faith alone in Christ alone. But the identification and description of the macrostructure of the covenants varied greatly.

Along with this idea was the identification of the "substance" of a given covenant. Simply put, two different substances are two different things—like wood and stone. The Reformed contrasted the covenant of works and the covenant of grace as differing in *substance* because they were built on or founded on two completely different things—law and gospel taken strictly. The substance of the covenant of works was normally identified as "do this and live." The substance of the covenant of grace was normally identified by the formula "I will be your God and you will be my people."[54] Once

---

[53] Reformed theology has approached this passage from both angles simultaneously. Historically, the mothers represent the church under two administrations. Dogmatically, they represent seeking justification through the law or the gospel (the covenant of grace vs. the covenant of works).

[54] The Particular Baptists considered this to be imprecise. They said that that was the formula for any covenant with God. For the Particular Baptists, the substance of the covenant of grace was salvation in Jesus Christ, or "I will remember your sins no more." This could be described in the formula "I will be

locked in to a definition of the substance of either covenant, theologians used them to sort and categorize the covenants of Scripture.

Cary fits within this methodology precisely.[55] Quoting John Owen, he said, "'So long as this Rule is retained, *Do this and live*, It is still the same Covenant for the Substance and Essence of it.' I can add no more after so worthy a Sentence from so worthy a Person."[56] For Cary, any covenant that operated on the principle of "do this and live," or any covenant that required working for blessing was the covenant of works. It was the same in substance. Thus for Cary, his concern was not simply that there were conditions in the Mosaic covenant, but that its reward was suspended upon obedience. For Flavel, a post-fall covenant of works was impossible.[57]

What remains to be clarified, however, is the relationship of Cary's position to his Particular Baptist brothers. Cary is quite strong in his identification of the Mosaic covenant with the covenant of works throughout the debate. Yet, while Cary affirmed that the Mosaic covenant was *the* covenant of works, often describing it in terms of being an edition of "Adam's covenant," and saying that it offered "life and salvation" he also acknowledged that *no one* could be saved by that covenant, and that this

---

your God . . . etc.", but not necessarily so. This led to quibbles over the use of the word "grace." The paedobaptists would call the post-fall covenant the covenant of grace. The Particular Baptists, agreeing that any post-fall covenant contained grace, would call the covenant of grace the covenant that promises forgiveness of sins to all its members, or the covenant of *saving* grace. John Tombes said in response to Stephen Marshall, "Is it equivocation in me to take the word *covenant of grace onely of the covenant of saving grace*? This is like as if a man should be charged with speaking nonsense, because he speakes good reason in right language." John Tombes, *An Apology or Plea for the Two Treatises, and Appendix to them Concerning Infant Baptisme* (London: Printed for Giles Calvert, 1646), 80. Italics original.

55 For Cary's use of Gal. 4:21 see Cary, *A Solemn Call*, 145.

56 Cary, *A Just Reply*, 51.

57 Each one was sticking to their definitions. Flavel considered Cary to be stubbornly seeing "Do this and live" as the reason why the Mosaic covenant was the covenant of works, while the Particular Baptists considered the paedobaptists to be stubbornly seeing "I will be your God and you will be my people" or "I will be a God to you and your seed after you" as the reason why the Abrahamic covenant was the covenant of grace.

impossibility made the Mosaic covenant *subservient* to the covenant of grace.[58] Flavel would not allow Cary to soften his position by ascribing subservience to the Mosaic covenant. For Flavel, this meant that there was a rival covenant to the covenant of grace after the fall.[59] Benjamin Keach defended Cary by saying, "*Adam's* Covenant, I grant, had one end and design, and the *Sinai* Covenant of Works had another; yet, may be, both, as to the Essence and Substance of them but one and the same Covenant: Which, doubtless, is all Mr. *Cary* intends."[60]

Cary's qualifications on subservience dull the sharpness of his views and bring him into line with the majority of his brothers on the purpose and design of the Mosaic covenant—it was not intended to justify, but to push hopeless and helpless sinners to Christ. Even so, many of his brothers did not express themselves to the extent that Cary had. It has been noted several times that it was a common Particular Baptist view that the Abrahamic and Mosaic covenants were connected covenants of works, but it was equally common to confine the covenants to an earthly, temporal, and typical context. In other words eschatological glory was not in view. With Galatians 4 in mind, it is not difficult to see where these emphases would come from. One of the contrasts mentioned by Paul is between that which is carnal, earthly, and temporary and that which is spiritual, celestial, and eternal. A few examples represent this position among the Particular Baptists.

Referring to the Abrahamic covenant of works, Thomas Patient said, "There is no promise of eternal life in it, but of temporal blessings in the Land of *Canaan*."[61]

Christopher Blackwood seems to combine the two views when he describes the Mosaic covenant as that in which "in the perfect observation whereof, (it's thought) they were to have *Canaan* here,

---

[58] Cary, *A Solemn Call*, 166-68.

[59] Flavel, *Vindiciae Legis & Fœderis: Or, A Reply to Mr. Philip Cary's Solemn Call* (London: Printed for M. Wotton, 1690), 23.

[60] Benjamin Keach, *The Ax laid to the Root Part II* (London: John Harris, 1693), 15.

[61] Thomas Patient, *A Treatise of Baptism*, 58.

and Heaven hereafter." Later he says, "The old Covenant was much upon temporall promises."[62]

Edward Hutchinson, quoting an unnamed author, describes Abraham's covenant as "'*The old Covenant (saith he) was a political Covenant made with the Jews. . . . God promises them his protection and that he would lead them to a fruitful land, overcome all their enemies, &c. with the like blessings.*'"[63]

Thomas Minge said:

> Here was *Abraham's* Call from his own Country, &c. and a promise of another Earthly Country, and the multiplication of his Seed that were to possess that Countrey (there was no other exprest than Earthly and Corporal, though thereby *Abraham* the Father of the Faithful, understood the Promise of the spiritual Seed and heavenly *Canaan* also).[64]

In light of these assertions, it should make sense that Owen was so appreciated by the Baptists. He also recognized the national and earthly character of Israel in the Mosaic covenant, and in the Baptists' opinion was very close in his analysis of Abraham's covenant as well.

Nehemiah Coxe, who so openly embraced Owen's views on the Mosaic covenant, said the following:

> In the Mosaical œconomy, there was such a remembrance of the Covenant of works revived, with the terms and sanction thereof; as that hereupon it is called the ministration of condemnation, and did ingender unto Bondage, *2 Cor. 3.7. Gal. 4.25.* But yet the promise of Salvation by the *Messiah*, being made long before, was not enervated thereby; but even this was laid in subserviency to

---

[62] Christopher Blackwood, *A Soul-Searching Catechism* (1658), 37, 40.

[63] Hutchinson, *A Treatise Concerning the Covenant*, 95-96.

[64] Thomas Minge, *Gospel-Baptism Or, Plain Proof, That the Mode of Dipping, Plunging or Immersion, now commonly used by the People called Anabaptists; is according to the Primitive Institution* (London: Printed by K. Astwood, 1700), 28. Italics original. In context, Minge is describing the Abrahamic covenant which he elsewhere specifically calls distinct from the covenant of grace. See Minge, *Gospel-Baptism*, 38.

> Gospel ends; and also the Gospel was preached to them, *Heb. 4.2.* (and so the covenant of grace revealed) though more darkly in types and shadows, through which they were instructed, to seek Justification unto Life by Christ promised, and so deliverance from the curse of the Law by him. Now amongst these some did believe, others did not; and so some were related to God in the New Covenant, others remained under the Old.[65]

Elsewhere, Coxe discusses man's state after the fall and says:

> In this Condition Man was altogether *helpless and without Strength*, being utterly disabled to stand before God upon Terms of a Covenant of Works. . . . And therefore it was impossible, not only that *this Covenant* now broken should be renewed with him, or any of his Posterity, for the same Ends, and in the same manner as it was at first made with upright Man.[66]

Coxe also stated concerning the Abrahamic covenant, of which the Mosaic covenant was an "enlargement," that it "Can give no more then *external and typical Blessings unto a Typical Seed*."[67]

Coxe's position that a "remembrance" of the covenant of works was "revived" in the Mosaic covenant is a much softer version of Cary's view of the Mosaic covenant, and perhaps the best articulation of the more common Particular Baptist stance on this question. While the vast majority of Particular Baptists affirmed the Abrahamic and Mosaic covenants to be covenants of works, most of them restricted the scope of the covenants themselves to national, earthly, typical spheres while also acknowledging that the promises and threats of the covenants of works were brought back to memory in certain ways. They all agreed, however, that the

---

[65] Nehemiah Coxe, *Vindiciae Veritatis Or A Confutation of The Heresies and Gross Errours Asserted by Thomas Collier In His Additional Word To His Body of Divinity* (London: Printed for Nath. Ponder, 1677), 78-79.

[66] Coxe, *A Discourse of the Covenants*, 35-36. Italics original.

[67] Coxe, *A Discourse of the Covenants*, 109. Italics original.

purpose of the Mosaic covenant was not to rival the covenant of grace but to push fallen mankind to Christ for salvation.[68]

So then, did they open the door for an alternative way of salvation for Old Testament believers? No they did not. Even the men who held the strongest of views on the Mosaic covenant, like Cary and Keach, made it clear that no one could be justified by the Mosaic covenant, and that this hopelessness made the covenant of works subservient to the covenant of grace.

In other words, to use the Particular Baptists' views on the Mosaic covenant to justify an alternate way of salvation in the Old Testament, you would first have to overcome their Calvinism and posit an upright human who can keep the law perfectly, and second you would have to prove that they considered the covenant of works, whether repeated or remade in the Mosaic covenant, to be coordinate, not subordinate, to the covenant of grace.[69] Connecting the Particular Baptists' views on these points to later dispensational thought would require a mutilation and distortion of their theology so complete that any and all resemblance would be destroyed in the process. Closer examination, as provided in the arguments above, demonstrates that the connections drawn in *A Puritan Theology* from the Particular Baptists to later "dispensationalist circles" are, in the

---

68 No Particular Baptist argued that there was a postlapsarian time when God was teaching men to seek justification by the works of the law as an end in itself. They all agreed on the postlapsarian subservience of the covenant of works, however they understood its relation to the Mosaic covenant.

69 Furthermore, it is misleading to attribute to the Particular Baptists the idea that after the fall the covenant of works, and thus a promise of eternal life, remained active and valid, albeit impossible. It was a standard argument within Reformed thought, even putting aside the web of views on the nature of the Mosaic covenant, that the law, remained a path of justification after the fall. This path, rather than justifying, condemned and sent sinners to the covenant of grace. Cf. Robert Rollock, *A Treatise of Effectual Calling* (London: Felix Kyngston, 1603), 21. "The couenant of works had this vse [to justify or condemn] in *Adam* before his fall. . . . After the fall, it hath the same vse in the the vnregenerate, elect, and reprobate, to wit, to iustifie and saue them, or to condemne them. And for as much as it can not iustifie them because of their corruption . . . it followeth that it must necessarilie condemne them."

words of Thomas Delaune, "no more to be found in the premises then a *Dolphin* in the *Woods*."[70]

Conclusion

In conclusion, debates tend to be unfruitful. Everyone wins. No one loses. Jones and Van Raalte have given us a glimpse into the thick and complicated debates between the Particular Baptists and their paedobaptists brothers, but their presentation of the Particular Baptists' side of the debate was lacking. It offered an incomplete picture of the Baptists' appropriation of John Owen, failing to see their use of his views on the Abrahamic covenant, not just the Mosaic covenant. They also arrived at false conclusions about the Particular Baptists by extrapolating Philip Cary's views too far, and thereby drawing false connections. The vast majority of Particular Baptists did not hold to an unconditional covenant of grace (nor did Cary really), many of them did not consider the Mosaic covenant to be *the* covenant of works, and they most certainly did not open the door for an alternate way of salvation in the Old Testament.

Particular Baptist covenant theology was not monolithic or uniform, nor was paedobaptist covenant theology. Each deserves careful thought and evaluation so as not to perpetuate the errors of the past. There is much that we can learn from those men, and from one another. And I can sincerely say with Nehemiah Coxe that there is, "nothing that my soul more longs for on Earth, than to see an intire and hearty Union of all that fear God, and hold the Head, however differing in their Sentiments about some things of lesser moment."[71]

---

[70] Delaune, *Truth Defended*, 17. Italics original. This is found in a postscript at the end of Delaune's work. The pagination reset at the beginning of the postscript.

[71] Coxe, *A Discourse of the Covenants*, v-vi.

CHRIST SPIRITUALLY PRESENT AND BELIEVERS SPIRITUALLY NOURISHED:

The Lord's Supper in Seventeenth-Century English Particular Baptist Life

G. Stephen Weaver, Jr.*

The eminent Baptist historian H. Leon McBeth was certainly correct in asserting that in the seventeenth century the "major controversy among Baptists concerned not the meaning of the Lord's Supper but eligibility to participate."[1] Since most discussions about the Lord's Supper in seventeenth-century Baptist life centered on who were the proper recipients rather than on the meaning of the Supper, there is comparatively much less data on Baptist views of the meaning of the Supper than one might suspect. For example, the earliest edition of the first confession of the Particular Baptists, the First London Confession of 1644, does not even mention the Lord's Supper at all. The 1646 edition added the words "and after to partake of the Lord's Supper" to the end of Article XXXIX which stated:

> That Baptisme is an Ordinance of the new Testament, given by Christ, to be dispensed onely upon persons professing faith, or

---

* G. Stephen Weaver, Jr., Ph.D., is senior pastor of Farmdale Baptist Church, Frankfort, KY. This article is adapted from his *Orthodox, Puritan, Baptist: Hercules Collins (1647-1702) and Particular Baptist in Early Modern England* (Göttingen: Vandenhoeck & Ruprecht, 2015).

[1] H. Leon McBeth, *The Baptist Heritage: Four Centuries of Baptist Witness* (Nashville: Broadman Press, 1987), 81. Consider, for example, the debate between William Kiffin and John Bunyan in the 1670s and 1680s. For more on this controversy, see Michael A. G. Haykin and C. Jeffrey Robinson, "Particular Baptist Debates about Communion and Hymn-Singing," in *'Drawn into Controversie': Reformed Theological Diversity and Debates Within Seventeenth-Century British Puritanism*, ed. Michael A. G. Haykin and C. Jeffrey Robinson (Göttingen: Vandenhoeck & Ruprecht, 2011), 285-96. The position of Collins and the Wapping Church on this important issue will be explored below.

> that are Disciples, or taught, who upon a profession of faith, ought to be baptized.[2]

This lack of attention to the Lord's Supper was most likely, as James M. Renihan has suggested, because it was not a matter of controversy among the Particular Baptists at this time. They assumed, rather than argued for, the meaning of the Lord's Supper. They most likely assumed a similar view of the Lord's Supper as "the Independents with whom they were companions."[3] Preliminary evidence that these early Baptists shared a common view of the meaning of the Lord's Supper with the Independents and Presbyterians is indicated by a comparison of their respective confessions of faith. The Savoy Declaration (Savoy) issued by the Independents in 1658 adopted unchanged the following statement from the Westminster Confession of Faith of 1647 (WCF).

> Worthy receivers outwardly partaking of the visible elements in this sacrament, do then also inwardly by faith, really and indeed, yet not carnally and corporally, but spiritually, receive and feed upon Christ crucified, and all benefits of his death; the body and blood of Christ being then not corporally or carnally in, with, or under the bread or wine; yet as really, but spiritually present to the faith of believers in that ordinance, as the elements themselves are to their outward senses.[4]

This same statement in essence was later officially adopted by the London Assembly of Particular Baptists in 1689,[5] but in the early

---

[2] Cf. 1st *LCF* XXXIX; *A Confession Of Faith Of seven Congregations or Churches of Christ in London* (1646), XXXIX. See also William L. Lumpkin, *Baptist Confessions of Faith*. 2nd ed. (Valley Forge, PA: Judson Press, 1969), 167.

[3] James M. Renihan, *Edification and Beauty: The Practical Ecclesiology of the English Particular Baptists, 1675–1705*, Studies in Baptist History and Thought 17 (Milton Keynes, England: Paternoster, 2008), 142.

[4] Philip Schaff, *The Creeds of Christendom, with a History and Critical Notes*, vol. 3, *The Evangelical Protestant Creeds, with Translations* (1931; repr., Grand Rapids: Baker Books, 2007), 666.

[5] The only difference being the 2LCF omits the phrase "in, with, or under the bread or wine; yet as really." James M. Renihan, *True Confessions: Baptist Documents in the Reformed Family* (Palmdale, CA: Reformed Baptist Academic Press, 2004), 185.

seventeenth century their view of the Lord's Supper is only implied through the circumstantial evidence. By the late seventeenth century, however, the Particular Baptists in London had begun to articulate more clearly their beliefs regarding the Lord's Supper. These views can be seen most clearly in two catechisms produced by the two Collins (Hercules and William) and in the Second London Confession of Faith (2LCF). After exploring these more representative sources, an examination will be undertaken of some of the writings of three of the more prominent Particular Baptist pastors in the latter half of seventeenth-century England. Before turning to the historical evidence, however, some important terms for this discussion need to be defined.

Defining Terms

Of the four major views on the Lord's Supper (i.e., transubstantiation, consubstantiation, spiritual presence, and memorial), only two have been considered as viable options for Baptists historically–spiritual presence and memorial. Millard J. Erickson has described the spiritual presence view as "the Calvinistic or Reformed view."[6] He asserts that this view "holds that Christ is present in the Lord's Supper but not physically or bodily. Rather his presence in the sacrament is spiritual or dynamic."[7] Participants in the Lord's Supper

> are spiritually nourished by partaking of the bread and the wine. The Holy Spirit brings them into closer connection with the person of Christ, the living head of the church and the source of spiritual vitality.[8]

According to this view, Christ is spiritually present and believers are spiritually nourished in the Lord's Supper. In the Baptist

---

This omission is most likely because the Lutheran view refuted by this phraseology was not really a threat in the English Particular Baptist community.

[6] Millard J. Erickson, *Christian Theology*, 2nd ed. (Grand Rapids: Baker Books, 2001), 1126.

[7] Erickson, *Christian Theology*, 1127.

[8] Erickson, *Christian Theology*, 1127.

expression of this view, believers receive spiritual nourishment and assurance of Christ's presence through their remembrance in faith of the once for all work of Christ on the cross. In contradistinction to the spiritual presence view, Erickson characterizes the memorial view, which he labels as the Zwinglian view, as "merely a commemoration" and as "essentially a commemoration of Christ's death."[9] This view emphasizes the importance of "bringing to mind the death of Christ and its efficacy on behalf of the believer."[10] Though this is also important to the spiritual view, the distinction is the lack of language emphasizing the presence of Christ and spiritual nourishment of believers. A good example of a modern expression of the memorial view is found in Article VII of the Baptist Faith and Message (2000). It says, "The Lord's Supper is a symbolic act of obedience whereby members of the church, through partaking of the bread and the fruit of the vine, memorialize the death of the Redeemer and anticipate His second coming."[11] This description is notable for what it does not say. Nothing of the spiritual presence of Christ or of the spiritual nourishment of believers is mentioned. The Lord's Supper is simply "a symbolic act" to "memorialize" the death of Christ.

Although Erickson's definitions will be employed in this chapter to distinguish between the Reformed view of spiritual presence and the modern-day Baptist view of the Lord's Supper as a memorial, his use of the term "Zwinglian" to refer to the memorial view is problematic. Interestingly, Erickson acknowledges that Zwingli may have actually held the view commonly referred to as "spiritual presence" and helpfully labels the view as "The Reformed View" instead of simply Calvin's view. Nevertheless, Erickson is inconsistent when he labels the memorial

---

[9] Erickson, *Christian Theology*, 1128.

[10] Erickson, *Christian Theology*, 1128.

[11] According to John Hammett, the use of the word "memorialize" indicates that the Baptist Faith and Message (2000) is articulating the memorial view. John S. Hammett, "Article VII: Baptism and the Lord's Supper" in *Baptist Faith and Message 2000: Critical Issues in America's Largest Protestant Denomination*, ed. Douglas K. Blount and Joseph D. Wooddell (Lanham, MD: Rowman & Littlefield Publishers, 2007), 77.

view as "The Zwinglian View." Although clarification is provided by Erickson, both in the text and footnotes, that Zwingli likely did not hold this view himself, the labeling is unhelpful and has no doubt led to further misunderstanding of Zwingli's actual views.[12] A careful study of Zwingli's writings on the Supper reveals much more than the common mischaracterization of his view.[13] In fact, both aspects noted by Erickson as constituting the Reformed view (spiritual presence of Christ and spiritual nourishment of believers) may be found in the Zwingli corpus. Zwingli's belief in the spiritual presence of Christ at the Supper is most clearly stated in the appendix to his *An Exposition of the Faith.*[14] Zwingli writes of the spiritual presence of Christ: "We believe Christ to be truly present in the Supper, indeed we do not believe that it is the Lord's Supper unless Christ is present."[15] Although Zwingli clearly affirms the presence of Christ at the Lord's Supper, it is not his physical body that is present. This was the major concern for Zwingli. He rejected any notion of the ubiquity of Christ's physical body. The physical body of Christ is seated at the right hand of the Father. Therefore,

---

[12] Erickson, *Christian Theology,* 1126-28. For helpful summary and analysis of Zwingli's actual writings on the Supper, see W. P. Stephens, *The Theology of Huldrych Zwingli* (Oxford: Clarendon Press, 1986), 180-93. Also see Bruce A. Ware, "The Meaning of the Lord's Supper in the Theology of Ulrich Zwingli (1484-1531)" in *The Lord's Supper: Remembering and Proclaiming Christ Until He Comes,* ed. Thomas R. Schreiner and Matthew R. Crawford, NAC Studies in Bible & Theology 10 (Nashville: B & H Academic, 2010), 229-47.

[13] Bruce Ware writes, "When we see the textured character of Zwingli's view, we must marvel at both its relative richness, when compared to popular reductionist (mis?)understandings of his position, and the striking similarities he shared with John Calvin's view of the Supper when compared to that of Martin Luther or of the Roman Catholic Church." Ware, "The Meaning of the Lord's Supper in the Theology of Ulrich Zwingli," 229.

[14] Originally written in Latin, the appendix was not included in G. W. Bromiley's English translation of "An Exposition of the Faith," in *Zwingli and Bullinger,* ed. G. W. Bromiley (Philadelphia: The Westminster Press, 1953), 239-79.

[15] "Christum credimus vere esse in coena; imo non credimus esse domini coenam nisi Christus adsit." Ulrich Zwingli, *Huldrici Zwingli Opera: Didactica Et Apologetica Ab Anno 1526 Usque Ad Obitum Auctoris Ceteraque Varia Poëtica Paedagogica Philologica Historica, Accedunt Sermones Vulgares in Psalmos Lingua Plerumque Vernacula,* ed. Melchior Schuler and Johanness Schulthess (Zürich: F. Schulthess, 1841), 4:73. English translation of this sentence found in W. P. Stephens, *Zwingli: An Introduction to His Thought* (Oxford: Clarendon Press, 2001), 106. I am indebted to Ian Hugh Clary for pointing out this statement.

Christ's presence at the Supper is spiritual, not physical. Because Christ is spiritually present, believers may feed upon Christ. Zwingli wrote that in the Lord's Supper "the natural and essential body of Christ in which he suffered and is now seated in heaven at the right hand of God is not eaten naturally and literally but only spiritually."[16] Later Zwingli explained what he means by stating that Christ is fed upon spiritually.

> To eat the body of Christ spiritually is equivalent to trusting with heart and soul upon the mercy and goodness of God through Christ, that is, to have the assurance of an unbroken faith that God will give us the forgiveness of sins and the joy of eternal salvation for the sake of his Son, who gave himself for us and reconciled the divine righteousness to us.[17]

Two sentences later, Zwingli succinctly summarized his point. "If I may put it more precisely, to eat the body of Christ sacramentally is to eat the body of Christ with the heart and the mind in conjunction with the sacrament."[18] In other words, the way in which believers are spiritually nourished through the Lord's Supper is by the believers' conscious awareness of the finished work of Christ symbolized through the physical elements of the Supper and their active faith that through this finished work their sins are forgiven. Perhaps the best summary of Zwingli's view on this subject is the following:

> So then, when you come to the Lord's Supper to feed spiritually upon Christ, and when you thank the Lord for his great favour, for the redemption whereby you are delivered from despair, and for the pledge whereby you are assured of eternal salvation, when you join with your brethren in partaking of the bread and wine which are the tokens of the body of Christ, then in the true sense of the word you eat him sacramentally. You do inwardly that which you represent outwardly, your soul being strengthened by the faith which you attest in the tokens.[19]

---

16 Bromiley, ed., *Zwingli and Bullinger*, 254.
17 Bromiley, ed., *Zwingli and Bullinger*, 258.
18 Bromiley, ed., *Zwingli and Bullinger*, 258.
19 Bromiley, ed., *Zwingli and Bullinger*, 259.

Clearly, Zwingli held to the two key components of the Reformed spiritual presence view of the Lord's Supper. His writings demonstrate that he affirmed both the spiritual presence of Christ and the spiritual nourishment of believers at the Supper. Thus, Zwingli was no "Zwinglian" in his view of the Lord's Supper.

Mark E. Dever has helpfully observed that of the four major views of the Lord's Supper (i.e., transubstantiation, consubstantiation, spiritual presence, and memorial), "only the Supper as *memorial* is universally accepted. Advocates for the other three positions go beyond the Supper as memorial, but no one denies this is an aspect of the Lord's Supper."[20] Dever went on to say, however, that

> Baptists have historically used language so rich about Christ's presence in the Lord's Supper for those who come by faith that little difference is perceptible between their position and the Reformed idea of Christ's spiritual presence.[21]

So when the *Baptist Faith and Message* (2000) calls the Lord's Supper "a symbolic act of obedience" by which believers "memorialize the death of the Redeemer," it is making a minimal statement meant to show common agreement among a sometimes diverse people.[22] All Baptists have, at the very least, believed in a memorial aspect of the Lord's Supper. Some, though, have used more expressive language to describe the spiritual benefits accrued through the remembrance of the death of Christ at the Supper. The evidence that the English Particular Baptists of the seventeenth century fall into this latter category will now be explored. An examination of the confessions, catechisms, and personal writings of these Baptists reveals that they held to the spiritual presence view of the Lord's Supper as defined above by Erickson as consisting of the following two aspects: the spiritual presence of Christ and the spiritual nourishment of believers.

---

[20] Mark E. Dever, "The Church," in *A Theology for the Church*, ed. Daniel L. Akin (Nashville: B&H Academic, 2007), 828.

[21] Dever, "The Church," 828.

[22] As noted above, the Heidelberg Catechism provided the same function on this very topic for the Reformed community in the sixteenth century.

Two Catechisms and a Confession

An excellent representative source for seventeenth-century English Particular Baptist views of the Lord's Supper is the catechisms and confessions which they wrote and circulated. Catechisms and confessions of faith reflect the perspective of a wider community than the writings of individual authors because they present truths commonly agreed upon and taught in the churches and homes. Therefore, the evidence cited from the two catechisms and confession of faith below should be given special attention.

1. Hercules Collins and *An Orthodox Catechism*

Some modern-day theologians might be surprised to learn that there is virtually no change between a sixteenth-century Reformed document and a seventeenth-century Baptist document on the issue of the Lord's Supper.[23] But that is exactly what one finds when the sections in the catechisms are examined side by side.[24] For example, the catechisms state that when a believer partakes of the Lord's Supper he may say,

> my soul is no less assuredly fed to everlasting life with his body, which was crucified for me, and his blood, which was shed for

---

[23] For example, see Thomas White, "A Baptist's Theology of the Lord's Supper" in *Restoring Integrity in Baptist Churches*, ed. Thomas White, Jason G. Duesing, and Malcolm B. Yarnell III (Grand Rapids: Kregel Publications, 2008), 148; also Brad Harper and Paul Louis Metzger, *Exploring Ecclesiology: An Evangelical and Ecumenical Introduction* (Grand Rapids: Brazos Press, 2009), 137. Although Gregg Allison notes in his recent monograph on ecclesiology that "the spiritual presence view of John Calvin . . . was embraced by many Baptists. Indeed, it was not until the end of the eighteenth century that the memorial view became predominant in Baptist churches." Gregg R. Allison, *Sojourners and Strangers: The Doctrine of the Church*, Foundations of Evangelical Theology (Wheaton, IL: Crossway, 2012), 385.

[24] The only real change of note between the two catechisms is the change of the title of the section from "Of the Holy Supper of Our Lord Jesus Christ" in the Heidelberg to "Of the Lord's Supper." This change was probably made because the former smacked of the High Anglicanism of the late seventeenth century. The opportunity to compare the two catechisms side by side is provided in Renihan, *True Confessions*, 239-87.

> me; than I receive and taste by the mouth of my body the bread and wine, the signs of the body and blood of our Lord, received at the hand of the minister.[25]

Further, the one who partakes of the body of Christ at the Lord's Table can be said to be made "more and more to be united to his sacred body, that though he be in heaven, and we on earth, yet nevertheless are we flesh of his flesh, and bone of his bones: and as all the members of the body are by one soul" through the work of "the Holy Ghost, who dwelleth both in Christ and us."[26] Likewise, Collins affirmed that in the Lord's Supper, "by this visible sign and pledge, he may assure us that we are as verily partakers of his body and blood, through the working of the Holy Ghost."[27] According to Michael Haykin, this statement means that Collins held that "although Christ's body is in heaven, we can have communion with the risen Christ in the Supper through the Spirit."[28] By retaining this language, Collins is assenting to the spiritual presence view of the Lord's Supper articulated by John Calvin.[29]

2. William Collins and *A Brief Instruction in the Principles of Christian Religion*

A second catechism was apparently produced by William Collins (d. 1702) around the year 1693 at the request of the General Assembly of Particular Baptists in England. Though often referred to as "Keach's Catechism," there is no evidence that Benjamin

---

[25] Hercules Collins, *An Orthodox Catechism* (London, 1680), 39; Renihan, *True Confessions*, 263.

[26] Collins, *An Orthodox Catechism*, 39; Renihan, *True Confessions*, 263-64.

[27] Collins, *An Orthodox Catechism*, 42; Renihan, *True Confessions*, 265.

[28] Michael A. G. Haykin, "'His soul-refreshing presence': The Lord's Supper in Calvinistic Baptist Thought and Experience in the 'Long' Eighteenth Century" in *Baptist Sacramentalism*, ed. Anthony R. Cross and Philip E. Thompson, Studies in Baptist History and Thought 5 (Milton Keynes, England: Paternoster Press, 2003), 181.

[29] See John Calvin, *The Institutes of the Christian Religion*, ed. John T. McNeill and trans. Ford Lewis Battles, *Library of Christian* Classics, vols. 20-21 (Philadelphia: Westminster Press, 1960), IV.vii.

Keach actually had a direct hand in forming this catechism.[30] Instead, the Assembly meeting in London in June of 1693 passed the following resolution:

> That a Catechism be drawn up, containing the substance of the Christian religion, for the instruction of children and servants, and that brother William Collins be desired to draw it up.[31]

Thus, it seems clear that it was William Collins, and not Benjamin Keach, to whom this catechism should be credited, which "defined what it was to be a Baptist throughout the eighteenth century, and for some years into the nineteenth."[32] Collins was uniquely gifted for such an important task.

William Collins, who served for twenty-nine years as the pastor of the Petty France church beginning in July of 1673 and ending at his death in October of 1702, was apparently widely recognized as both a theologian and a scholar.[33] Ivimey states that his "eminence . . . as a scholar and theologian was very great."[34] In his funeral sermon, John Piggott called Collins "a very learned and judicious minister of Christ."[35] He then elaborated on the learning achieved by Collins:

> 'Twas early that he discovered an inclination to study and books, and his progress in learning was swift and sure. When he had passed through learning, and had had the approbation of one of the most severe critics of this age (Dr. Busby), he began to travel and, if I mistake not, before that time, God had made him sensible of sin, and drawn him to his Son. When he came abroad, not going so far as he at first designed, he remained a considerable time in

---

[30] See Tom J. Nettles, *Teaching Truth, Training Hearts: The Study of Catechisms in Baptist Life* (Amityville, NY: Calvary Press Publishing, 1998), 49; and Austin Walker, *The Excellent Benjamin Keach* (Dundas, ON: Joshua Press, 2004), 219; both of which dispel this common assumption.

[31] Joseph Ivimey, *A History of the English Baptists* (London: Printed for the Author, 1811), 1:533.

[32] Nettles, *Teaching Truth, Training Hearts*, 47.

[33] William Collins died the same month of the same year as Hercules Collins.

[34] Ivimey, *A History of the English Baptists*, 3:332.

[35] John Piggott, *Eleven sermons preach'd upon special occasions* (London: John Darby, 1714), 279.

> France and Italy; where he finished the course of his other studies preparatory to that of Theology, to which he closely applied himself upon his return to England. . . . I need not say how well he was prepared for the study of divinity by nature, learning, and grace, for his proficiency therein soon appeared; and after he had passed a little time preaching in the country, he had a very remarkable call by this church.[36]

Collins was a man whose remarkable gifts were all used in the service of the One who had so obviously gifted him.

William Collins' early commitment to studying theology served him well in the years which followed. On August 26, 1677, an obscure reference is made in the minutes of the Petty France church to the publication of a Confession of Faith.[37] This is commonly believed to be the same confession which would become known as the Second London Confession of Faith when reissued in 1689. If this is the case, there is little doubt that William Collins and Nehemiah Coxe, who served as Collins' assistant at Petty France for the first sixteen years of his pastorate, were the chief architects of this historic document which continues to unite Particular Baptists today. It should not be surprising therefore, that this same William Collins was requested to produce a catechism expounding the confession which he had originally produced.

Just as *An Orthodox Catechism* was an adaptation of the Heidelberg Catechism, *A Brief Instruction in the Principles of Christian Religion* was an adaptation of the Westminster Assembly's Shorter Catechism.[38] It was published with the desire, according to "An Advertisement to the Reader," "to shew our near Agreement with many other Christians, of whom we have great Esteem."[39] The differences, though "being not much,"[40] are again what one might expect from a Baptist revision of a Reformed document. William Collins, like Hercules Collins, modifies the section on baptism.

---

36 Piggott, *Eleven sermons*, 279.

37 *Petty France Church Minute Book*, 6.

38 See Schaff, *The Creeds of Christendom*, 3:676-704.

39 *A Brief Instruction in the Principles of Christian Religion*, 5th ed. (London, 1695), 24.

40 *A Brief Instruction*, 24.

However, unlike *An Orthodox Catechism*, *A Brief Instruction* removes the use of the word sacrament, replacing it with "Baptism and the Lord's Supper" or "Ordinance."[41] Notwithstanding this change in terminology, *A Brief Instruction* retains an exposition of the ideas intended by the Westminster divines' use of the word sacrament. For example, in answer to the question, "What are the outward Means, whereby Christ communicateth to us the Benefits of Redemption?," the catechism includes baptism and the Lord's Supper along with the Word and prayer as means that "are made effectual to the Elect for Salvation."[42] Likewise, in answer to the question, "How do Baptism and the Lord's Supper, become effectual Means of Salvation?," this Baptist catechism follows the Shorter Catechism in saying these "become effectual Means of Salvation, not for any virtue in them, or in him that doth administer them, but only by the Blessing of Christ, and the working of the Spirit in those that by Faith receive them."[43] Clearly, the Lord's Supper was seen as more than a memorial, but what benefits are conferred to those who receive the Lord's Supper in a worthy manner? According to the catechism, "the worthy Receivers are, not after a Corporal and Carnal manner, but by Faith, made Partakers of his Body and Blood, with all his Benefits, to their spiritual Nourishment, and growth in Grace."[44] This understanding of the spiritual nourishment of believers communicated by Christ through the Holy Spirit distinguishes this catechism's view of the Lord's Supper from the memorial view and places it squarely within a Reformed understanding of spiritual presence.

3. Second London Confession of Faith

The 2LCF was first published in 1677, but was officially adopted by the London General Assembly in 1689.[45] It would eventually be

---

[41] Compare *SC* Q. 88, 91, and 96 with *A Brief Instruction*, questions 93, 96, and 102 respectively.

[42] *A Brief Instruction*, 18.

[43] *A Brief Instruction*, 19.

[44] *A Brief Instruction*, 20.

[45] *A Narrative of the Proceedings of the General Assembly Of divers Pastors, Messengers and Ministring Brethren of the Baptized Churches, met together in London,*

republished in 1699 with a list of those who signed the document on behalf of their churches at this historic gathering.[46] Hercules Collins and William Collins, along with men like Hanserd Knollys, William Kiffin, and Benjamin Keach, were among the original signers of this historic document. This confession, like the two catechisms discussed above, had its origins in a Reformed document, this time the WCF.[47] The framers of the 2LCF explained their rationale for following the WCF and the Savoy so closely in their introductory letter "To the Judicious and Impartial Reader." It reads:

> we did in like manner conclude it best to follow their example in making use of the very same words with them both, in these articles (which are very many) wherein our faith and doctrine is the same with theirs. And this we did, the more abundantly to manifest our consent with both, in all the fundamental articles of the Christian religion, as also with many others, whose orthodox confessions have been published to the World, on the behalf of the protestants in diverse nations and cities; and also to convince all, that we have no itch to clog religion with new words, but to readily acquiesce in that form of sound words, which hath been, in consent with the holy scriptures, used by others before us; hereby declaring before God, angels, & men, our hearty agreement with them, in that wholesome protestant doctrine, which with so clear evidence of scriptures they have asserted. Some things, indeed, are in some places added, some terms omitted, and some few changed; but these alterations are of that nature, as that we need not doubt, any charge or suspicion of unsoundness in the faith, from any of our brethren upon the account of them.[48]

Like the *Orthodox Catechism* and *Brief Instruction*, the 2LCF changed

---

from Septemb. 3. To 12. 1689, from divers parts of England and Wales: Owning the Doctrine of Personal Election, and final Perseverance (London, 1689), 18.

[46] *A Confession of Faith, Put forth by the Elders and Brethren Of man Congregations of Christians (Baptized upon Profession of their Faith) in London and the Countrey*. 3rd ed. (London: S. Bridge, 1699), back cover. This confession may also be accessed in Lumpkin, *Baptist Confessions of Faith*, 235-95.

[47] See Schaff, *The Creeds of Christendom*, 3:600-73.

[48] *A Confession Of Faith* (1677), "To the Judicious and Impartial Reader;" Lumpkin, *Baptist Confessions of Faith*, 245-46.

the sections on baptism. This confession also exchanged the word "sacrament" for "ordinance."[49]

The 2LCF does not deny that one purpose of the Lord's Supper is to serve as a "perpetual remembrance" of the death of Jesus. However, the confession says more than this. It also states in the first paragraph of chapter XXX that the Supper is for the "confirmation of the faith of believers in all the benefits" of Christ's death. Indeed, chapter XXX of the 2LCF does present the Lord's Supper according to a spiritual presence view in two important ways: as "spiritual nourishment" to believers and Christ as "spiritually present."[50] The confession states that believers receive "spiritual nourishment" by the "Supper of the Lord Jesus."[51] This idea of "spiritual nourishment" is important in distinguishing the position of this confession from a memorial only perspective, but perhaps the clearest evidence that it articulates a spiritual presence view of the Supper is seen in paragraph seven of chapter XXX.

> Worthy receivers, outwardly partaking of the visible elements in this ordinance, do then also inwardly by faith, really and indeed, yet not carnally and corporally, but spiritually receive, and feed upon Christ crucified, and all the benefits of his death; the body and blood of Christ being then not corporally or carnally, but spiritually present to the faith of believers in that ordinance, as the elements themselves are to their outward senses.[52]

Throughout chapter XXX, the confession is careful to reject any Roman Catholic understanding of the Supper. This is seen in paragraph seven as the believer's feeding upon Christ and Christ's spiritual presence are both said not to be taken "carnally or corporally," but spiritually. Nevertheless, the 2LCF affirms that

---

[49] For an analysis of the "minimal" differences between the confessions on the Lord's Supper, see Michael A. G. Haykin, *Kiffin, Knollys and Keach: Rediscovering our English Baptist Heritage* (Leeds, England: Reformation Today Trust, 1996), 78-79.

[50] *A Confession Of Faith* (1677), 98-102; Lumpkin, *Baptist Confessions of Faith*, 291-93.

[51] *A Confession Of Faith* (1677), 98-99; Lumpkin, *Baptist Confessions of Faith*, 291.

[52] *A Confession Of Faith* (1677), 102; Lumpkin, *Baptist Confessions of Faith*, 293.

believers "really and indeed, . . . receive, and feed upon Christ crucified," albeit "spiritually." Likewise Christ is said to be "spiritually present to the faith of believers in that ordinance." No further evidence should need to be given to prove that the English Particular Baptists of the seventeenth century held to a spiritual presence view of the Lord's Supper than this representative document signed by thirty-seven pastors on behalf of "upwards of one hundred baptized congregations in England and Wales (denying Arminianism)."[53]

The 2LCF, like the two catechisms examined above, articulates a spiritual presence view of the Lord's Supper by asserting both the spiritual nourishment of believers and the spiritual presence of Christ at the Supper.[54]

Kiffin, Knollys, and Keach

Although no further evidence is needed to prove that the English Particular Baptists of the seventeenth century held a spiritual presence view of the Lord's Supper, in the interest of a thorough treatment of the subject, a final locus of evidence will be examined. This final source of evidence to be considered is the individual writings of three of the most prominent English Particular Baptist pastors of the seventeenth century—William Kiffin, Hanserd Knollys, and Benjamin Keach. Though none of the three wrote works directly addressing the meaning of the Lord's Supper, there is a spattering of references to the meaning of the Supper in their writings. These will now be examined in order to ascertain if they reflect a memorial or spiritual presence view of the Supper.

---

[53] *A Confession Of Faith* (1699), back cover; Lumpkin, *Baptist Confessions of Faith*, 238-39.

[54] Thus, E. P. Winter was wrong to state, based on the confession's omission of the word sacrament, that: "Clearly, at least some Baptist would not be bound to accept 'Calvinist' sacramental doctrine." E. P. Winter, "Calvinist and Zwinglian Views of the Lord's Supper Among the Baptists of the Seventeenth Century," *BQ* 15, no. 7 (July 1954): 325.

1. William Kiffin

Nineteenth-century English Baptist historian Joseph Ivimey called William Kiffin (1616-1701) "one of the most extraordinary persons whom the denomination has produced, both as to the consistency and correctness of his principles and the eminence of his worldly and religious character."[55] High praise, but an examination of the life of this remarkable individual seems to bear out Ivimey's assessment.[56] Kiffin was orphaned as a child, apprenticed to a glover as a young man, and eventually became one of the wealthiest merchants in England. His longevity, Kiffin's life spanned most of the seventeenth century, allowed him to be the only individual who was an original signer of both the 1644 and 1689 London confessions of faith.[57] Kiffin's standing as a leading statesman for his fellow Particular Baptists was augmented by the fact that for over sixty years Kiffin served as the pastor of the Baptist congregation which met at Devonshire Square in London.[58] William Kiffin was most certainly "extraordinary."

Kiffin wrote an important tract on the Lord's Supper, but its main focus was on who were its rightful participants/receivers. In *A Sober Discourse of Right to Church-Communion*, Kiffin argued against John Bunyan (who held to open membership and open communion) [59] that only believers baptized by immersion are the proper recipients of communion, i.e., "no unbaptized person may

---

[55] Joseph Ivimey, *The Life of Mr. William Kiffin* (London, 1833), xi.

[56] For details on the life of Kiffin, see B. A. Ramsbottom, *Stranger Than Fiction. The Life of William Kiffin* (Harpenden, England: Gospel Standard Trust, 1989); and Haykin, *Kiffin, Knollys and Keach*, 42-52.

[57] Hanserd Knollys would sign the second edition (1646) of the First London Confession, along with the 2LCF in 1689.

[58] A history of the Devonshire Square church up to the early nineteenth century is include in Walter Wilson, *The History and Antiquities of the Dissenting Churches* (London, 1808), 1:400-54.

[59] These two ideas were almost always linked in seventeenth-century thought. In other words, while there were sometimes Separatist or Baptist congregations which were open communion, they were also invariably open membership. At the same time, those churches which restricted membership to baptized believers, also restricted communion to the same.

be regularly admitted to the Lord's Supper.[60]" Though Kiffin's focus in this work was on who may be admitted to church membership and the table of communion, he did address the nature of the Lord's Supper in at least two places. First, while arguing for the priority of baptism before the Lord's Supper in the life of the believer, Kiffin described baptism as "the Sacrament of Spiritual *Birth*" and the Lord's Supper as the sacrament of "Spiritual *Nourishment* and *Growth*" by which believers are "*Spiritually fed.*"[61] Notice that Kiffin does not shy away from using the term "sacrament" to describe baptism and the Lord's Supper. He, like Hercules Collins in his *An Orthodox Catechism,* obviously had no problem with this word when properly defined.[62] Kiffin's argument was that baptism is an initiatory rite for a believer at the beginning of spiritual life and the Lord's Supper is an ongoing rite of spiritual nourishment and growth as a believer. Kiffin's understanding of the Lord's Supper as a means of spiritual nourishment and growth by which believers are spiritually fed had implications for his argument that baptism should precede the Lord's Supper. A couple of pages later, Kiffin addressed the nature of the Lord's Supper a second time in his argument that "*Baptism Signs* and *Seals* our Salvation to us" by appealing to the assumed common understanding that "the *Supper* is a Spiritual participation of the *Body and Blood* of Christ by Faith, and so (not meerly by the work done) is a means of Salvation."[63] In other words, Kiffin is arguing that the Lord's Supper provides spiritual communion with Christ by faith in the same way that baptism "signs" and "seals" our salvation, not because of any merit in the act itself, but by symbolizing the work of Christ which confirms our faith in him. Kiffin's point here was to show the importance of baptism (which, of course, is defined as immersion) for the professing believer. For the interest of this chapter, it is sufficient to see that by using the language of "spiritual nourishment" and "spiritual participation"

---

60 William Kiffin, *A Sober Discourse of Right to Church-Communion* (London: Geo. Larkin, 1681), title page.

61 Kiffin, *A Sober Discourse*, 23.

62 See the definition of this term found above in the section "The Sacraments."

63 Kiffin, *A Sober Discourse*, 25.

Kiffin assumed a spiritual presence view of the Lord's Supper as he argued that believer's baptism by immersion was a necessary prerequisite to the Supper.

2. Hanserd Knollys

Like William Kiffin, the life of Hanserd Knollys (c. 1599-1691)[64] spanned most of the seventeenth century. Knollys was unusual for a Baptist in that he was university educated. The son of a priest in the Church of England, Knollys studied at St. Catherine Hall in Cambridge University.[65] Hanserd followed his father Richard as a minister in the Church of England at the parish church at Humberstone in Lincolnshire.[66] After resigning his parish in 1631 over his Puritan convictions, Knollys had completely broken with the national church by 1635. By 1644, Knollys had come to Baptist convictions and signed the second edition (1646) of the First London Confession of Faith.[67] Knollys was highly regarded in the Particular Baptist community as a scholar. He was a prolific author producing manuals on Latin, Greek, and Hebrew, as well as numerous expositions of Scripture.[68] In his exposition of the first chapter of the Song of Solomon, Knollys draws on the imagery of the love relationship between the king and the spouse to expound the love of God for his people. One aspect of this relationship is the table fellowship which Knollys applied to the communion of Christ with believers in the Lord's Supper.

Jay T. Collier has analyzed Hanserd Knollys approach to interpreting Scripture and has found him to use a fourfold method:

---

[64] For biographical sketches of Knollys, see Dennis C. Bustin, *Paradox and Perseverance: Hanserd Knollys, Particular Baptist Pioneer in Seventeenth-Century England* (Milton Keynes, England: Paternoster, 2006); Pope A. Duncan, *Hanserd Knollys: Seventeenth-Century Baptist* (Nashville: Broadman Press, 1965); and Haykin, *Kiffin, Knollys and Keach*, 54-61.

[65] Duncan, *Hanserd Knollys*, 1-3.

[66] Haykin, *Kiffin, Knollys and Keach*, 54.

[67] Haykin, *Kiffin, Knollys and Keach*, 54-55.

[68] Jay T. Collier, "Hanserd Knollys as interpreter of Scripture: An examination of his An Exposition of the First Chapter of the Song of Solomon" in *Eusebeia: The Bulletin of The Jonathan Edwards Centre for Reformed Spirituality* 5 (Autumn 2005): 6.

typically, each section began by announcing the verses to be treated, gave a synopsis of the argument or aim of the text, and then alternated between commenting on the meaning of words or phrases and improving upon these comments with meditations.[69]

Knollys' comments related to the Lord's Supper fall under this last category of meditations. Each meditation had "at least a statement of a doctrine" and often "application for his readers."[70] By examining his meditations, Knollys' doctrine of the Lord's Supper and its application to believers will become evident.

Reflecting on Song of Solomon 1:8 ("feed thy kids beside the shepherds' tents"), Knollys called the church the place where "faithful Ministers dispense his holy Ordinances" that believers might "be fed and nourished, converted and comforted, sanctified and saved by the Spirit and grace of God in Jesus Christ."[71] Knollys also identified the church and the kingdom very closely. In his meditation on Song of Solomon 1:12 ("While the king sitteth at his table"), Knollys stated that the table in Christ's kingdom is the Lord's Table where Christ is in communion with believers.

> This Kingdome is his Church, the Keyes whereof he gave unto his Apostles, Mat. 16. 18, 19. And his Table in his Kingdome is the Lords Table, to wit, his holy Ordinances (especially that of the Lords Supper. 1 Cor. 10.21. Called *the Lords Table*) where Christ sits and Sups with his Saints.[72]

Elsewhere, Knollys expressed similarly:

> Christ and his Saints, do enjoy mutual communion and spiritual fellowship one with another, at the Lords Supper. . . . Christ Sups with his Saints, and the Saints Sup with Christ, in his holy Ordinances.[73]

---

[69] Collier, "Hanserd Knollys as interpreter of Scripture," 16.

[70] Collier, "Hanserd Knollys as interpreter of Scripture," 23.

[71] Hanserd Knollys, *An Exposition of the First Chapter of the Song of Solomon* (London: W. Godbid, 1656), 39.

[72] Knollys, *An Exposition of the First Chapter of the Song of Solomon*, 56.

[73] Knollys, *An Exposition of the First Chapter of the Song of Solomon*, 57.

The marriage bed was also an image of spiritual communion for Knollys. When the Song of Solomon 1:15 says, "also our bed is green," Knollys saw an application to the ordinances which are "the means of Grace wherein Christ and his Saints have spiritual communion together."[74] Clearly, Knollys believed that Christ was spiritually present with believers at the Supper, but does he also proffer a notion of spiritual nourishment for believers?

The evidence shows that Knollys not only articulated a belief in the spiritual presence of Christ at the Lord's Supper, he also held that believers were spiritually nourished by the bread and wine. In his meditation on the table imagery of Song of Solomon 1:12, Knollys stated, "Christ giveth his Saints spiritual Bread, hidden Manna, New-wine and water of life at his Supper."[75] Since there is spiritual nourishment provided to believers at the Supper, Knollys urged believers not to neglect this ordinance.

> The Saints when they sup with Christ, have meat and drink, which others know not of. Those beleevers, who sleight or neglect any of the holy Administrations and Ordinances of God, do want that fellowship with the Father, and that communion with Jesus Christ in the Spirit, which other beleevers do enjoy.[76]

Knollys then moved from the doctrine that believers are nourished at the Supper to an exhortation to believers. Knollys here directly addressed his readers:

> O dear Freinds [*sic*]! Be not wanting to your precious souls, either in sleighting or neglecting the Ordinances of God, why should you cry, O my leanness, my barrenness &c? . . . How unkindly do ye deal with Christ, to sleight and neglect or refuse his gracious Invitations, to heavenly banquets at his Table?[77]

Apparently this was a matter of some importance to Knollys. The seriousness with which Knollys views an abstention from the

---

[74] Knollys, *An Exposition of the First Chapter of the Song of Solomon*, 78.
[75] Knollys, *An Exposition of the First Chapter of the Song of Solomon*, 57.
[76] Knollys, *An Exposition of the First Chapter of the Song of Solomon*, 57.
[77] Knollys, *An Exposition of the First Chapter of the Song of Solomon*, 57-58.

Lord's Supper flows from his high understanding of the table as a place where Christ is spiritually present and at which believers are spiritually nourished.

3. Benjamin Keach

Murdina MacDonald has called Benjamin Keach (1640-1704)[78] "the single most important apologist for Calvinistic Baptist views in the period 1689-1702."[79] He was prolific as an author, no other Baptist of the period comes close to matching Keach's productivity. Originally a General Baptist, Keach became convinced of a Calvinistic soteriology within five years of arriving in London where he had brought his family in order to escape persecution.[80] At some point, Keach met Kiffin and Knollys, and when he remarried in 1672 two years after his first wife had died, it was Knollys who officiated at the wedding.[81] This, perhaps, explains the influences which prompted Keach's mysterious shift to the Particular Baptist camp. In the same year as his second marriage, Keach began a church in Horsleydown, Southwark, which he served as pastor until his death in 1704.[82]

Among Keach's numerous writings is his ΤΡΟΠΟΛΟΓΙΑ: *A Key to Open Scripture Metaphors*, which, as the title suggests, provides a guide to interpreting the metaphors and types found in Scripture.[83] This work includes an exposition of the scriptural teaching on the Lord's Supper in which Keach rejects the Roman Catholic

---

[78] For biographical sketches of Keach, see Haykin, *Kiffin, Knollys and Keach*, 83-97; and Austin Walker, *The Excellent Benjamin Keach* (Dundas, ON: Joshua Press, 2004).

[79] Murdina MacDonald, "London Calvinistic Baptists 1689-1727: Tensions Within a Dissenting Community Under Toleration" (D.Phil. thesis, Regent's Park College, Oxford University, 1982), 77.

[80] Walker, *The Excellent Benjamin Keach*, 389.

[81] Haykin, *Kiffin, Knollys and Keach*, 86.

[82] This is the same congregation later famously served by John Gill and Charles Haddon Spurgeon, and that still exists as the Metropolitan Tabernacle in London.

[83] B[enjamin] K[each] ΤΡΟΠΟΛΟΓΙΑ: *A Key To Open Scripture Metaphors* (London: J. D., 1681). This work is now in print as Benjamin Keach, *Preaching from the Types and Metaphors of the Bible* (Grand Rapids: Kregel Publications, 1972). The modern edition will be used for citation purposes below.

understanding of transubstantiation. He seems to be the most cautious of any of the Particular Baptist authors in addressing the nature of the Lord's Supper. He is careful not to use terminology that would imply a literal, physical presence of Christ at the Supper. Christ, Keach declared, used "metaphorical and figurative expressions . . . when he instituted the holy sacrament of the Supper."[84] The language used by Christ in the institution of the Supper was metaphorical, and the phrase "This is my body" should not be interpreted literally as if Christ is corporally present. Despite these cautions, however, there is evidence that Keach held to more than a memorial view of the Supper. For example, he could say of the Supper, "There is a mystical conveyance or communication of all Christ's blessed merits to our souls through faith held forth hereby, and in a glorious manner received, in the right participation of it."[85] Keach clearly believed that something happens spiritually between believers and Christ in the proper observance of the Lord's Supper. A memorialist would not say this. Furthermore, Keach said something that only one who had endured the trials of persecution possibly could. He wrote that the Supper "may animate and encourage us to suffer martyrdom, when called to it, for his sake."[86] There is a real strengthening that comes to those who observe the Supper in faith.

Further evidence of Keach's understanding of the Lord's Supper is found in the articles of faith adopted by the Horsleydown congregation.[87] As pastor, Keach led his church to adopt the confession of faith which he had compiled. In it he included the Lord's Supper as a means of grace, in Article XX, "Of the Means of Grace."

> We believe that the outward and more ordinary means, whereby Christ communicates to us the Benefits of Redemption, are his Holy Ordinances, as Prayer, the Word of God, and Preaching,

---

[84] Keach, *Preaching from the Types and Metaphors*, 632.
[85] Keach, *Preaching from the Types and Metaphors*, 639.
[86] Keach, *Preaching from the Types and Metaphors*, 639.
[87] Benjamin Keach, *The Articles of Faith of the Church of Christ, or Congregation meeting at Horsley-down, Benjamin Keach, Pastor, As asserted this 10th of the 6th Month, 1697* (London, 1697).

> with Baptism, and the Lord's Supper, &c. and yet notwithstanding it is the Spirit of God that maketh Prayer, Reading, &c. and specially the Preaching of the Word, effectual to the convincing, converting, building up, and comforting, through Faith, all the Elect of God unto Salvation.[88]

For Keach, one of the means by which "Christ communicates to us the Benefits of Redemption" was the Lord's Supper. This is accomplished by the Spirit who makes all the means of grace "effectual to the convincing, converting, building up, and comforting, through Faith." This high view of the Lord's Supper is also seen in Article XXIV "Of the Lord's Supper."

> [The Lord's Supper] . . . [is] appointed for our spiritual Nourishment, and Growth in Grace, and as a farther Engagement in, and to all Duties we owe to Jesus Christ, and as a Pledg of his eternal Love to us, and as a Token of our Communion with him, and one with another.[89]

Once again, the language of spiritual nourishment and growth is used as a benefit of the Lord's Supper. Even with Keach's more guarded use of language, it is clear that he held to a view of the Lord's Supper more akin to the spiritual presence view than the memorial only view.

Eligible Participants of the Supper

Before ending this discussion of the Lord's Supper, a word needs to be said regarding its proper recipients. As noted above, this was the major issue of debate among seventeenth-century Baptists and deserves some treatment here. This is especially the case since some have argued that the Wapping Church practiced open communion and that Collins taught the same.[90] In his dissertation on the

---

[88] Keach, *The Articles of Faith*, 19.

[89] Keach, *The Articles of Faith*, 24-25.

[90] In a recent essay, New Testament scholar Ray Van Neste has stated that "the first Particular Baptist church, under pastors John Spilsbury and Hercules Collins, practiced open Communion." Ray Van Neste, "The Lord's Supper in the Context

doctrine of the Lord's Supper among English Baptists, Glenn O. Hilburn described Spilsbury, the first pastor of the Wapping Church, as "an ardent advocate of open communion principles."[91] This put the author in the unenviable position of having to argue that Spilsbury's beliefs were in direct contradiction to the confession of faith which was published with his signature in 1646.[92] Unfortunately, this is not the only challenge which Hilburn faces. His analysis of Spilsbury's works is marred by a misunderstanding of the historical context and how the term "communion" was used in the seventeenth century.[93] First, Hilburn does not properly deal with those whom Spilsbury is addressing in his two extant works.[94] Spilsbury's first work on baptism was largely apologetic, the majority of it being a response to objections made by paedobaptists who saw believer's baptism as a novel practice. Since Spilsbury also affirmed covenant theology, his work interacted, as Thomas J. Nettles has noted, "of necessity" with the covenant theology of his paedobaptist contemporaries. Spilsbury argued "that the spirituality of the new covenant in Christ eliminated the possibility of an infant's participation in it."[95] By

---

of the Local Church" in *The Lord's Supper: Remembering and Proclaiming Christ Until He Comes*, ed. Thomas R. Schreiner and Matthew R. Crawford, 385. Van Neste is following a 1960 dissertation on English Baptists and the Lord's Supper and an 1860 monograph on the open communion controversy among the Baptists of Norwich. Glenn O. Hilburn, "The Lord's Supper: Admission and Exclusion Among English Baptists" (Th.D. thesis, Southwestern Baptist Theological Seminary, 1960); and George Gould, *Open Communion and the Baptists of Norwich* (Norwich, England: Josiah Fletcher, 1860).

[91] Hilburn, "The Lord's Supper," 44.

[92] *A Confession of Faith Of seven Congregations or Churches of Christ in London, which are commonly (but unjustly)called Anabaptists*, 2nd ed. (London: Matth. Simmons, 1646), "To the judicious and impartial Reader." This confession added the phrase "and after to partake of the Lords supper" to article XXXIX of the confession that dealt with baptism. Hilburn states that Spilsbury's signature upon this confession proves that one did not have to affirm "close communion" to affirm the confession. Hilburn, "The Lord's Supper," 44.

[93] Hilburn, "The Lord's Supper," 50-54.

[94] Cf. John Spilsbury, *A Treatise Concerning the Lawfull Subject of Baptism* (London: Henry Hills, 1652); and John Spilsbury, *Gods Ordinance, the Saints Priviledge* (London: M. Simmons, 1646).

[95] Thomas J. Nettles, *The Baptists: Key People Involved in Forming a Baptist Identity*, vol. 1, *Beginnings in Britain* (Fearn, Scotland: Christian Focus Publications, 2005), 1:113.

missing this important point of historical context, Hilburn insists that Spilsbury was merely arguing that baptism was not what constituted a church and therefore, he assumes, Spilsbury does not require baptism before the Lord's Supper. In reality, Spilsbury's point was that baptism does not form the church, rather baptism symbolizes the spiritual reality experienced by those included in the covenant of grace through faith. Ironically, Hilburn takes a selection out of context from Spilsbury which makes exactly this point. He writes, "Baptism was said to be a symbol of 'the parties regeneration and spirituall new birth' and not an initiatory rite."[96] The full quote from Spilsbury reads:

> To Baptize Infants, makes the holy ordinance of God a lying signe, because none of those things can be expected in an Infant which the said ordinance holds forth or signifies in the administration thereof, which is the parties regeneration and spirituall new birth; a dying and burying with Christ in respect of sin, and a rising with him in a new life to God, and a confirmation of faith in the death and resurrection of Christ, and a free remission of sinne by the same; as *Rom.* 6. 3, 4. *Col.* 2. 12. I *Pet.* 3. 21. *Act*: 2. 38. None of all which can be expected in an Infant.[97]

This hardly seems to be a plea for allowing those baptized as infants to participate at the Lord's Table.

Similarly, in his analysis of Spilsbury's *Gods Ordinance, the Saints Priviledge,* Hilburn fails to account for the historical context. Whereas Spilsbury's first work was largely a response to objections made by paedobaptists, this work responded to the objections of another group, the Seekers. This group argued that the true church has been lost during the time of Roman dominance in the church and therefore the ordinances were likewise lost. They were "seekers" of a restoration of primitive Christianity by a new Pentecost with living Apostles. The early American Baptist Roger Williams had been influenced by this movement about the same time as Spilsbury wrote this tract. Spilsbury responded to the influential arguments of the Seekers by stating that every believer

---

[96] Hilburn, "The Lord's Supper," 51.

[97] Spilsbury, *A Treatise Concerning the Lawfull Subject of Baptisme*, 26.

has the right to the ordinances which have been purchased by Christ. That he was addressing Seekers is clear from his words in the letter to the reader.

> And thus in summe, Christian Reader, I present to thy view the subject I deale upon, endeavering to maintaine the right & priviledges purchased by Christ, and freely given to all that believe in him for salvation, against such as oppose the same: who under pretense of seeking the truth, doe by cunning and craftie enquiries undermine the same, and (as they of old did) overthrow the faith of some: who deny unto such as do believe in Jesus Christ for eternal life, Church fellowship and communion with Christ in his Ordinances of the new Testament, for want (as they say) of a Ministery with power from God to call and fit a people for Ordinances, and to administer the same.[98]

Hilburn does not acknowledge this historical background, instead arguing that Spilsbury is continuing "to deny the necessity of baptism for church membership and communion."[99] Ironically, this second work by Spilsbury included a letter "To the Reader" by Benjamin Coxe, whom Hilburn himself classifies as a close membership, strict communion Baptist.[100] Hilburn does not mention this connection. Obviously, Coxe would not have endorsed this work if it was indeed arguing against his own position.

In addition to the errors of historical background, Hilburn also fails to distinguish the way the word "communion" was used in seventeenth-century Baptist literature. James Renihan has demonstrated conclusively that the Baptists of the period used the term "communion" to refer to relationships between members of the churches or between churches in association with one another.[101] Hilburn, as many have done, seems to assume that "communion" always refers to the Lord's Supper. This is rarely, if

---

98 John Spilsbury, *Gods Ordinance, the Saints Priviledge*, "To the Reader."

99 Hilburn, "The Lord's Supper," 53.

100 See Hilburn, "The Lord's Supper," 64-66.

101 See James Renihan's analysis of the use of this term in the confessions, ecclesiological writings, associational records, documents of the general assembly and church minute books of seventeenth-century Baptists. Renihan, *Edification and Beauty*, 156-73.

ever, the case. Because of the misunderstanding of his use of the term, Hilburn assumes that when Spilsbury says "a church is onely so a church before Baptisme, as that the end of her union, is for communion,"[102] he is arguing that the church may have the Lord's Supper before having baptism. However, if the word is being used to refer to the fellowship that exists between Christ and each member of the congregation, Hilburn's conclusion does not follow. Most glaring in Hilburn's misreading of this term is when he cites Spilsbury's personal confession of faith stating his belief

> that there is an holy and blessed communion of Saints, that God of his grace calls such as belong to life by election, unto the fellowship of his Sonne by the Gospel; of which matter, God by his Word and Spirit joyns them together in his covenant of grace, and so constitutes his Church.[103]

The expression "communion of Saints" seems most naturally interpreted in the same sense as when it appears in the Apostle's Creed, as the fellowship of all believers, past, present, and future.[104] However, Hilburn concludes, "Therefore, Spilsbury held that the only stipulation for church membership and communion was Christian conversion. Baptism was important but not prerequisite to Lord's Supper participation."[105] This conclusion is not warranted by the evidence. It is based on a misreading of both the historical context and the meaning of the word "communion" in early English Baptist thought.

---

[102] Hilburn omits without ellipsis "onely so" and incorrectly capitalizes "communion." Cf. Hilburn, "The Lord's Supper," 51; and Spilsbury, *A Treatise Concerning the Lawfull Subject of Baptisme*, 41. Hilburn was apparently relying upon George Gould's citation of this work since the identical reading appears in Gould, *Open Communion and the Baptists of Norwich*, cxix. Gould's note on the prior page that "I regret to say that I have failed to obtain this book" is quite damaging to Hilburn's thesis. Gould, *Open Communion and the Baptists of Norwich*, cxviii. This dependence upon a secondary source which did not itself have access to the actual work being cited is sufficient explanation for why the original work has been so misused by Hilburn.

[103] Spilsbury, *A Treatise Concerning the Lawfull Subject of Baptisme*, 44.

[104] For a summary of how this doctrine was understood by the early church, see Robert Louis Wilken, *The Spirit of Early Christian Thought: Seeking the Face of God* (New Haven, CT: Yale University Press, 2003), 46-48.

[105] Hilburn, "The Lord's Supper," 51.

In like manner, Hilburn has also misread Collins on the communion question. Hilburn asserts that "Spilsbury's influence was such that his church at Old Gravel Lane, Wapping continued to practice open communion and probably open membership."[106] He admits that Collins, whom he calls "an ardent advocate" of the immersion of believers, "may have possibly altered the open membership practice." Hilburn claims, however, that he did not "regard immersion as prerequisite for communion."[107] Hilburn is here once again clearly following Gould, who cited Collins' treatment of the Lord's Supper in his *An Orthodox Catechism* as evidence that Collins taught open communion.

> Q. *Who are to come to the Table of the Lord?*
> A. They only, who are truly sorrowful they have offended God by their Sins, and yet trust that those Sins are pardoned them for Christ's sake, and what other Infirmities they have, that those are covered by his Passion and Death; who also desire more and more to go forward in Faith and Integrity of life: but Hypocrites, and them which do not truly repent, do eat (b) and drink Damnation to themselves.
> (b) 1 Cor. 10.21. and 11.28, &c.
> Q. *Are they also to be admitted to the Lord's Supper who in Confession and Life declare themselves to be Infidels, profane, and ungodly?*
> A. No; For by that means the Ordinance of God is profaned, and the Wrath of God is (c) stirred up against the whole Assembly, wherefore the Church by the Commandment of Christ and his Apostles, inspired by the Holy Ghost using the Keys of the Kingdom of Heaven, ought to drive them from this Supper till they shall repent and change their Manners.
> (c) 1 Cor. 11.20, 34. Isa. 1.11, &c. and 66.3. Jer. 7.21, &c. Psal. 50.16, &c.[108]

Gould summarized these questions and responses in the following words.

> All the faithful, or, in other words, all penitents who trusted in Christ for pardon were free to come unto the Table of the Lord,

---

[106] Hilburn, "The Lord's Supper," 54.
[107] Hilburn, "The Lord's Supper," 54.
[108] Collins, *An Orthodox Catechism*, 43-44; Renihan, *True Confessions*, 266; and Gould, *Open Communion and the Baptists of Norwich*, cxxvi-cxxvii.

> and none were excluded but those who in Confession and Life declared themselves Infidels, profane, and ungodly.[109]

Therefore, he concluded that it is "inconceivable that a Strict Communionist should be the author of such statements."[110] Does this conclusion bear up to scrutiny in light of the historical evidence?

Gould seems to be unaware that *An Orthodox Catechism* was an adaptation of the Heidelberg Catechism of 1563.[111] This is an important point for interpreting this document correctly. One of the reasons given by Collins for the publication of his catechism was to identify himself and his fellow Particular Baptists as a part of the Reformed community throughout Europe. Collins thus noted in his preface, "I concenter with the most Orthodox Divines in the Fundamental Principles and Articles of the Christian Faith."[112] As Collins further wrote:

> albeit there are some differences between many Godly Divines and us in Church-Constitution, yet inasmuch as those things are not the Essence of Christianity, but that we do agree in the fundamental Doctrine thereof, there is sufficient ground to lay aside all bitterness and prejudice, and labor to maintain a spirit of Love each to other, knowing we shall never see all alike here.[113]

Both the choice of the Heidelberg as the basis for his catechism and the use of the word "orthodox" in the title highlight Collins' interest in identifying himself with historic Protestant orthodoxy. As Renihan writes of Collins' choice of a title:

> While it obviously refers to the true character of the doctrines it promotes, it also identifies the source of those doctrines, the so-called Protestant Orthodox divines of Europe. Collins was making

---

109 Gould, *Open Communion and the Baptists of Norwich*, cxxvii.
110 Gould, *Open Communion and the Baptists of Norwich*, cxxvii.
111 There is no mention of this fact in either Gould or Hilburn.
112 Collins, *An Orthodox Catechism*, "Preface;" Renihan, *True Confessions*, 237.
113 Collins, *An Orthodox Catechism*, "Preface;" Renihan, *True Confessions*, 237.

an emphatic statement: just as they are Orthodox, so also are we.[114]

Given Collins' purpose in utilizing this historic Reformed document, we can understand that he is merely reproducing, almost completely unchanged, questions 81 and 82 of the Heidelberg Catechism.[115] Collins' desire to show unity with the wider Reformed community causes him to alter the catechism as little as possible. Nevertheless, Collins was not unwilling to modify the Heidelberg where he thought it absolutely essential.

The most noticeable change made by Collins in his catechism is the change of the section dealing with baptism. Collins' desire to promote unity between Baptists and other Protestant groups did not cause him to compromise this Baptist distinctive. In fact, in his preface which calls for unity on the "Essence of Christianity," Collins stated that he only differed with the "Orthodox Divines" in "some things about Church-constitution, wherein I have taken a little pains to show you the true form of God's House."[116] The first hint within the catechism that Collins would make a significant change on the subject of baptism is found when he inserts the phrase "figured out in holy Baptism" into the answer to question 43 of the Heidelberg.[117] This answer describes the believer's sharing with Christ in his crucifixion, death, and burial. Collins' insertion of the phrase about baptism demonstrates the importance of the symbol's correspondence to the thing signified for seventeenth-century Baptists.

Although the questions describing the meaning of baptism remain unchanged in the *Orthodox Catechism*, Collins has added a complete section on the mode and proper subjects of baptism. This illustrates that the Baptist quarrel with their Reformed brothers and sisters was not so much over the understanding of the meaning of baptism (at least as it applied to adults). Their disagreement was

---

114 Collins, *An Orthodox Catechism*, "Preface;" Renihan, *True Confessions*, 235.

115 This section of the two catechisms can be compared side-by-side in Renihan, *True Confessions*, 266.

116 Collins, *An Orthodox Catechism*, "Preface;" Renihan, *True Confessions*, 237.

117 Collins, *An Orthodox Catechism*, 16; Renihan, *True Confessions*, 248.

over the mode of baptism and the identity of the sacrament's appropriate recipients. In answer to the question, "What is Baptism?"—which is conspicuous by its absence in the Heidelberg—Collins essentially reproduced the description of baptism from the 2LCF, which had first appeared three year earlier in 1677: "Immersion or dipping of the Person in Water in the Name of the Father, Son, and Holy Ghost, by such who are duly qualified by Christ."[118] Having answered the question of mode with this definition, this answer begged the question, "Who are the proper subjects of this ordinance?" The response came almost word for word from the 2LCF: "Those who do actually profess Repentance towards God, Faith in, and Obedience to our Lord Jesus Christ."[119] The only difference between the *Orthodox Catechism* and the 2LCF is that Collins adds the word "Christ." Collins continued his treatment of baptism by denying the validity of the baptism of infants based upon the fact that Scripture nowhere commands it.[120] This is followed by a series of questions providing an extensive rebuttal of arguments for infant baptism from covenant theology.[121] From this point on, Collins resumed following the Heidelberg in its treatment of the meaning of baptism. The discussion of the mode and proper recipients of baptism thus constitutes the main area of divergence between the two catechisms. Having already settled the question of baptism, Collins apparently saw no need to address the issue further in the section on the Lord's Supper. This was not an oversight on his part, but merely reflects that he, like the framers of the Heidelberg Catechism, believed that only the baptized may partake of the Lord's Supper.[122] Their only difference on this point

---

[118] Collins, *An Orthodox Catechism*, 26; Renihan, *True Confessions*, 255. Cf. the 2LCF 29.3-4.

[119] Collins, *An Orthodox Catechism*, 26; Renihan, *True Confessions*, 255. See the 2LCF 29.2.

[120] Collins, *An Orthodox Catechism*, 26-27; Renihan, *True Confessions*, 255.

[121] Collins, *An Orthodox Catechism*, 27-31; Renihan, *True Confessions*, 255-58.

[122] John Hammett notes: "Most denominations agree that baptism should normally precede participation in the Lord's Supper. For those that practice infant baptism, the order seems obvious. The problem is that Baptists do not see infant baptism as baptism at all." John S. Hammett, *Biblical Foundations for Baptist Churches: A Contemporary Ecclesiology* (Grand Rapids: Kregel Publications, 2005), 283.

was as to what constituted baptism. Understanding the provenance of this document should cause one to beware of basing an interpretation of Collins' beliefs on the proper recipients of the Lord's Supper solely upon a selection out of context from this document.

Thankfully, Collins did say more addressing the topic of who may receive the Lord's Supper. In his *Some Reasons for Separation from the Communion of the Church of England,* he rebuked his hypothetical Conformist antagonist for the practice of the Church of England of making infants members of the church, yet withholding the Lord's Supper from them. In a string of rebuttals of the liturgy of the Church of England, Collins included,

> you make Infants Members of the Church, Article 27.[123] and yet deny them the Eucharist, the Apostles gave the Eucharist to all that were Members, therefore would not admit Infants to be Members, because the same Qualifications which are prerequisite to the Lords Supper, the same is required to Baptism.[124]

By calling out the national church for inconsistency on this manner, Collins seems to be articulating a view which linked church membership, baptism, and the Lord's Supper. The apostolic pattern, which these early Baptists were committed to following, was to restrict church membership to adult professors of faith who had been immersed as believers. Thus, those baptized as infants were permitted neither to church membership nor the Lord's Table.

---

123 A reference to Article 27 of the Thirty-Nine Articles of the Church of England which states: "Baptism is not only a sign of profession, and mark of difference, whereby Christian men are discerned from others that be not christened, but it is also a sign of Regeneration or New-Birth, whereby, as by an instrument, they that receive Baptism rightly are grafted into the Church; the promises of the forgiveness of sin, and of our adoption to be the sons of God by the Holy Ghost, are visibly signed and sealed, Faith is confirmed, and Grace increased by virtue of prayer unto God.

The Baptism of young Children is in any wise to be retained in the Church, as most agreeable with the institution of Christ."

124 Hercules Collins, *Some Reasons for Separation From the Communion of the Church of England, and the Unreasonableness of Persecution Upon that Account* (London: John How, 1682), 13.

That this was the practice of the Wapping Church is apparent from an examination of the minute book. The church only received members upon their baptism,[125] upon assurance of their good standing in another church practicing believer's baptism,[126] or from a paedobaptist church after assurances had been provided of the individual's baptism.[127] Furthermore, reception into membership was required before permission to partake of the Lord's Supper was granted. Members were typically received by the church on the day on which they observed the Lord's Supper.[128] This was most likely done in order to allow them to partake of the Supper upon their entry into church membership. On May 23, 1683, just three years after the publication of *An Orthodox Catechism,* the minute book provides an example of the practice of the Wapping Church in receiving members at the Lord's Table.

> It was agreed by the Church in old gravell lan that Such Persons that propound themselves for Communion: before they are Received, it Shall be Signified both ther name and place of Abod to the Church the next Day of that the Church break bread that we may have a mutuiall Satisfaction before they are admitted.[129]

---

[125] E.g., see *Wapping Church Book,* 2 June 1691. "Att Thee Same Time It was Agreed after full Satisfaction of the work of Grace & of the Life & Conversation Mistris Jones That Shee haveing Been Baptized Is Ordered to Bee Received Into full Communion The next first Day."

[126] E.g., see *Wapping Church Book,* 4 August 1696. "Att a Church meeting then held it was agreed that Mary Cattell formerly a member of the Congregation whereof Mr. Wiles is pastor be receved into full Communion of this Congregation They having first sent to that congregation & having receved sattisfaction from them that she was in full Communion with them."

[127] E.g., see *Wapping Church Book,* 21 November 1693. "It was further agreed that Bro Lindsey and Bro Evans be sent as messengers to Mr Burgis Minister at [Westminster?] to inquire of him wether John Thomas be in full communion with that congregation where he is the elder." [Below in pencil: "satisfaction being given was baptized"]. Also, see *Wapping Church Book,* 19 June 1696. The church agreed to receive a sister as member who was "formerly baptized by B^{r} Belshen."

[128] This appears to have normally been once a month, although sometimes this schedule was altered. See *Wapping Church Book,* 29 September 1696. "It was further agreed that the Church alter the day of ther breaking bread & to be next first day come 3 weakes in respect of the benefit of the moone."

[129] *Wapping Church Book,* 23 May 1683.

Nearly ten years later, another record collaborates this practice and also provides evidence of the care taken in receiving new members into the church.

> Brother Burgis of Colechesther was last breaking bread day Received in as a member of our Society upon the evidence and testimony of severall Baptized persons and since that have had a letter testimoniall with many hands which gives Ample sattisfaction.[130]

There is no evidence of any persons not immersed partaking of the Lord's Supper at the Wapping Church. Instead, the evidence points in a different direction; namely, that the Wapping Church required confirmation of baptism and church membership before allowing participation at the Lord's Table.

Conclusion

While most modern discussions of the nature of the Lord's Supper assume that the Baptist view is that the Supper is merely a memorial, a closer examination of the historical data reveals that the most prominent writing Particular Baptists of the seventeenth century, along with the confessional statements and catechisms they helped to formulate, articulated a spiritual presence view. This is the view expressed in the two catechisms produced by Hercules and Williams Collins respectively, as well as the view found to be articulated in the 2LCF. The individual writings of three giants of seventeenth-century Baptist life were also examined and the same conclusion was reached for each. These men were not memorialists. They believed that when Christ's sacrifice was remembered at the Supper, Christ was spiritually present to the believer and that the believer received strength and nourishment from his communion with Christ. While the memorial view would eventually come to dominate in Particular Baptist church life by the late eighteenth century, the earliest Particular Baptists understood the Lord's

---

[130] *Wapping Church Book*, 24 January 1693.

Supper to be a rich experience of Christ's nearness and the believer's nourishment through the Spirit when received in faith. For Collins and the Wapping Church, baptism by immersion was a prerequisite both to church membership and the Lord's Supper.

ETERNAL CREATOR OF TIME

James E. Dolezal*

Augustine of Hippo famously wrote, "What, then, is time? If no one asks me, I know; if I want to explain it to someone who asks me, I do not know."[1] Perplexing as the reality of time is, it is even more puzzling to contemplate the eternality of its Creator. "You have made all eras of time and you are before all time," Augustine states. Yet, he observes, God is not "earlier in time" than all eras of time.[2] Time brings nothing new to him.

> Your years do not come and go. Our years pass and new ones arrive only so that all may come in turn, but your years stand all at once, because they are stable: there is no pushing out of vanishing years by those that are coming on, because with you none are transient . . . [Y]our today does not give way to tomorrow, nor follow yesterday. Your Today is eternity.[3]

God is eternally before all time, and yet is not time's *temporal* antecedent. This is mystery to be sure, though one historically upheld by orthodox Christians.

Reformed theologians traditionally welcomed this mystery of God's eternality as a source of wonder and motive for worship. John Owen declares:

> How inconceivable is this glorious divine property unto the thoughts and minds of men! How weak are the ways and terms

---

*James E. Dolezal, Ph.D., is part-time professor of theology, philosophy, and church history at Cairn University, Langhorne, PA, and author of *God without Parts: Divine Simplicity and the Metaphysics of God's Absoluteness* (Eugene, OR: Pickwick Publications, 2011).

[1] Augustine, *The Confessions*, trans. Maria Boulding (Hyde Park, NY: New City Press, 1997), bk. XI, ch. 14.

[2] Augustine, *Confessions*, bk. XI, ch. 13.

[3] Augustine, *Confessions*, bk. XI, ch. 13.

> whereby they go about to express it. . . . He that says most only signifies what he knows of what it is not. We are of yesterday, change every moment, and are leaving our station to-morrow. God is still the same, was so before the world was, — from eternity. And now I cannot think what I have said, but only have intimated what I adore.[4]

The incomprehensibility of divine eternality need not reduce believers to silence or hopeless agnosticism. Owen allows that theologians may speak of this perfection, even if in a predominantly negative mode, signifying what it is not, and he specifically indicates that eternality is not change. In other words, while we may not be able to form an adequate positive concept of God's eternity in our minds, we should at least be willing to affirm that time produces no change in God. Herman Bavinck captures the basic conviction of the classical eternity doctrine when he identifies its three basic marks as excluding in God "a beginning, an end, and the succession of moments."[5] God is not subject to the passage of moments. This is what Owen finds worthy of adoration.

Yet this classical eternalist[6] doctrine has undergone a considerable amount of scrutiny in the past 40 years. Many modern philosophers and theologians, including numerous evangelicals, have elected to either abandon or significantly modify the classical doctrine. There are undoubtedly many motives for this, including: the supposed philosophical incoherence of the doctrine; new theories about the nature of time; the alleged lack of biblical support for atemporality; and the proclivity of certain forms of biblical theology to consider every actor in Scripture as an historical individual, including God. Among Christian theologians the greatest challenge seems to be the question of how an eternal God

---

[4] John Owen, *A Practical Exposition Upon Psalm CXXX*, in *The Works of John Owen*, ed. William H. Goold, vol. 6 (1850-53; reprint, Edinburgh: The Banner of Truth Trust, 2000), 6:622.

[5] Herman Bavinck, *Reformed Dogmatics*, ed. John Bolt, trans. John Vriend, 4 vols. (Grand Rapids: Baker Academic, 2004), 2:162.

[6] The term "eternal" and its variants will be used to refer to the notion of timelessness or atemporality as distinct from all temporalist conceptions of God.

could create time[7] and providentially act in time in a meaningful way without being temporal in some respect. Responses to this challenge vary from those that deny divine atemporality altogether to those that seek to augment it with a measure of divine temporalism.

One way of framing this challenge may be to ask the question: Did God *become* Creator of heaven and earth, or is he such eternally? It is the reaffirmation of the latter, as the historic Reformed position, that motivates the present article.[8] I shall first consider three different alternatives to the classical eternity doctrine and endeavor to show that the rejection of eternal creatorhood is one of the most significant common denominators shared among them. Next, I will survey some of the fundamental features of the classical doctrine in order to demonstrate the orthodox intentions underlying it and to spotlight where it differs from the recent revisionist accounts. Finally, I will return to the consideration of God as eternal Creator of time and seek to show that the confession of this truth is a mystery that has historically been upheld and must remain so today if we are to consistently maintain divine eternity. If we can find a way to confess that God's act of creation is eternal, then it seems that one of the most significant motivations for adopting divine temporalism will have been eliminated.

Contemporary Dissent from the Eternity Doctrine

There is no single alternative put forth by those who oppose the traditional eternity doctrine. Some scholars forsake it entirely, while others still retain some of its features, though with important

---

[7] Properly considered, time is not an entity or an essence but rather is merely a relation between things that change and are liable to change. Time is concreated with all creatures insofar as it is the measure of all their movement. When we speak of time as a realm we do not mean to imply that it is like a container or box in which temporal things exist, rather we denote simply the created order which is populated by beings that are subject to and undergo change and thus are measured temporally.

[8] A similar undertaking from a more philosophical perspective can be found in Paul Helm, "Eternal Creation," *Tyndale Bulletin* 45 (1994): 321-38.

modifications. The three views surveyed here are: (1) the temporal God view; (2) the timeless-turned-temporal God view; and (3) the timeless-and-temporal God view. It is not my aim to offer a thorough investigation of each of these views. Many of the arguments advanced by the authors mentioned are highly sophisticated and would demand far more detail than is called for in the purposes of this article. What should be observed is that each of these positions finds God's relationship to the world to be an insuperable obstacle to maintaining the traditional teaching.

1. Temporal God

Christian advocates of divine temporality do not propose that God began to exist at some point in time, but rather that he perpetually passes through a succession of temporal moments. Nicholas Wolterstorff, a leading advocate of this position, prefers to characterize God as "everlasting" as opposed to eternal. He makes a case for divine temporality in his highly influential 1975 article, "God Everlasting."[9] His first argument against the eternalist doctrine is that the Bible presents God as acting in history:

> Indeed, so basic to the biblical writings is their speaking of God as an agent within history that if one viewed God as only an impassive factor in reality, or as one whose agency does not occur within human history, one would have to regard the biblical speech about God as at best one long sequence of metaphors pointing to a reality for which they are singularly inept, and as at worst one long sequence of falsehoods.[10]

His second criticism is a subspecies of the first, specifically, that a God who redeems must necessarily be temporal. Man's need of

---

[9] Nicholas Wolterstorff, "God Everlasting," in *God and the Good: Essays in Honor of Henry Stob*, ed. Clifton J. Olebeke and Lewis B. Smedes (Grand Rapids: Eerdmans, 1975), reprinted in Brian Davies, ed., *Philosophy of Religion: A Guide and Anthology* (Oxford: Oxford University Press, 2000), 485-504. Cf. Nicholas Wolterstorff, "Unqualified Divine Temporality," in *God and Time: Four Views*, ed. Gregory E. Ganssle (Downers Grove, IL: IVP Academic, 2001), 187-213.

[10] Wolterstorff, "Everlasting God," 485.

salvation is due to the historical reality of the fall and the divine accomplishment of that salvation must unfold on that same historical plane of reality. Thus,

> . . . if we are to accept this picture of God as acting for the renewal of human life, we must conceive of him as everlasting rather than eternal. God the Redeemer cannot be a God eternal. This is so because God the Redeemer is a God who *changes*. Any being which changes is a being among whose states there is temporal succession.[11]

Wolterstorff acknowledges that God may be unchanging in his faithfulness to his redemptive purposes; but he denies that God is *ontologically* changeless.

Wolterstorff's concern is rather straightforward. Some things God does in history succeed other things he does. Therefore, as there is a sequence of divine effects there must be something about the divine actor that allows him to begin to do what he previously did not and to cease doing what he once did. Surely God does not speak to Moses from the burning bush at the same moment in time as he parts the Red Sea waters. The latter follows after the former. Wolterstorff asks, "And does not this sort of succession constitute a change on God's time-strand—not a change in his 'essence,' but nonetheless a change on his time-strand?"[12]

Yet another component of Wolterstorff's case for divine temporality is drawn from his consideration of God's knowledge of temporal events and his plans for those events. If God is to truly know temporal events then he must know them as temporally past, present, or future. If he did not then he would not be aware of whether the event was occurring *now* or if it had already passed or was yet to come. There is a great difference, for example, between knowing that the Japanese attacked Pearl Harbor on December 7, 1941 and knowing that the Japanese attack on Pearl Harbor is *occurring now*. The latter could only be known by someone whose act of knowledge was temporally indexed and simultaneous to the

---

[11] Wolterstorff, "Everlasting God," 485. Emphasis his.

[12] Wolterstorff, "Everlasting God," 495.

event known. Thus, for God to know temporal indexicals, such as past, present, and future, his act of knowing must itself be able to undergo movement from the past, though the present, to the future. Furthermore, insofar as the biblical writers depict God as remembering past events it must be the case that his act of remembrance follows in time the event remembered. "For one can only remember that *e* [an event] has occurred after *e* has occurred."[13] God's act of remembering cannot be eternal inasmuch as what he remembers is not eternal.

As for planning, Wolterstorff understands it to be the case that all plans temporally precede the things planned. "For consider some event which someone brings about," he writes, "and suppose that he planned to bring it about. His planning to bring it about must occur before the planned event occurs. For otherwise it is not a case of planning."[14] The conclusion Wolterstorff draws is that an eternal God cannot know that an event has occurred, is occurring, or will occur; he cannot remember an event; and he cannot plan to bring about an event and do so. But as each of these actions is essential to the biblical writers' presentation of God as creator and redeemer, it seems that God as he is depicted in Scripture is "fundamentally noneternal" and in fact is "fundamentally in time."[15]

Wolterstorff sums up his argument as follows:

> [T]he biblical presentation of God presupposes that God is everlasting rather than eternal. God is indeed without beginning and without end. But at least some of his aspects stand in temporal order-relations to each other. Thus God, too, has a time-strand. His life and existence is itself temporal. . . . Further, the events to be found on God's time-strand belong within the same temporal array as that which contains our time-strands. God's aspects do not only bear temporal order-relations to each other but to the aspects of created entities as well. And the aspects and succession of aspects to be found on God's time-strand are such

---

[13] Wolterstorff, "Everlasting God," 500.
[14] Wolterstorff, "Everlasting God," 500.
[15] Wolterstorff, "Everlasting God," 501.

> that they constitute *changes* thereon. God's life and existence incorporates changeful succession.[16]

Perhaps we can distill the basic logic of Wolterstorff's argument in the following manner. Intelligent agents who produce a variety of sequential effects must be capable of sequential acts of agency and knowledge. Inasmuch as a thing acts and knows according to its manner of being, the agent who sequentially produces and knows new temporal effects must necessarily exist in a sequential fashion, that is, temporally. If the agent has any knowledge of his temporal effects it must be a temporally indexed knowledge. When Wolterstorff penned his article 40 years ago he was distinctly self-conscious that he was upholding the minority viewpoint. Since that time scores of Christian theologians have joined the temporalist ranks.[17]

2. Timeless-turned-temporal God

William Lane Craig espouses the view of God put forth by the straight temporalist position, though with a significant caveat. He does not believe that God was temporal prior to the creation of the world.[18] If God existed before time and creation, as Craig believes the Bible intimates in passages such as Proverbs 8:22-23, 2 Timothy 1:9, Titus 1:2-3, and Jude 25, then it must be the case that God was once timeless in some respect.[19] On the other hand, once God

---

[16] Wolterstorff, "Everlasting God," 503.

[17] See, for example, John S. Feinberg, *No One Like Him* (Wheaton, IL: Crossway Books, 2001), 375-436; Thomas V. Morris, *Our Idea of God: An Introduction to Philosophical Theology* (Notre Dame, IN: University of Notre Dame Press, 1991), 119-38; William Hasker, "The Absence of a Timeless God," in *God and Time: Essays on the Divine Nature*, ed. Gregory E. Ganssle and David M. Woodruff (Oxford: Oxford University Press, 2002), 182-206.

[18] See William Lane Craig, "Timelessness and Omnitemporality," in *God and Time: Four Views*, 129-60; William Lane Craig, *Time and Eternity: Exploring God's Relationship to Time* (Wheaton, IL: Crossway Books, 2001); J. P. Moreland and William Lane Craig, *Philosophical Foundations for a Christian Worldview* (Downers Grove, IL: IVP Academic, 2003), 511-15.

[19] Craig, "Timelessness and Omnitemporality," 131-32.

creates the world he seems to enter new relations as Creator and Sustainer and it is difficult to imagine that he could exist in such relations without being touched by the temporality of the world itself. Craig explains this motive for affirming divine temporality:

> God could have never stood in those relations, had he so willed. But by virtue of his creating a temporal world, God comes into a relation with the world the moment it springs into being. Thus even if it is not the case that God is temporal prior to his creation of the world, he undergoes an extrinsic change at the moment of creation which draws him into time in virtue of his real relation to the world.[20]

Craig finds convincing arguments on both sides of the temporalist and eternalist debate. Yet he does not believe both could be true of God at once. It must be the case, he concludes, that God's eternity gave way to temporality at the moment of creation. He states his basic claim quite simply: "With the creation of the universe, time began, and God entered into time at the moment of creation in virtue of his real relations with the created order. It follows therefore that God must be timeless without the universe and temporal with the universe."[21] Craig is aware that his view appears to require that there are two phases of God's life, a timeless and a temporal, with the timeless phase being chronologically earlier than the temporal. But he rejects that this is what his view actually amounts to inasmuch as describing the timeless phase as "earlier than" the temporal phase ascribes a temporal designation to timelessness itself, which is logically incoherent. Whatever we are to make of this claim, and many find this qualification of Craig's view incoherent, it does seem clear that he does not regard God to be presently eternal since his real relation to the world necessarily requires him to act and think temporally and thus to exist temporally. Since God is no longer without the world, but with it, he must be temporal and no longer timeless.

---

[20] Craig, "Timelessness and Omnitemporality," 141.
[21] Craig, "Timelessness and Omnitemporality," 156.

3. Timeless-and-temporal God

Another temporalist view that dissents from the two previous versions is one in which God is conceived as *both* timeless and temporal. Though in agreement with the timeless-turned-temporal view on many points, proponents of this position differ from it in that they do not believe God forfeited his eternity when he assumed temporality. Rather, his temporal manner of being is added to him in a way that augments, rather than displaces, his essential timelessness. Advocates of the various forms of this argument are desirous to preserve a true confession of God's timeless eternity. Yet, as with the stronger forms of temporalism, they too find the fact of God's relation to the world as Creator and Redeemer a compelling reason to affirm that God must exist and act temporally, at least in some qualified respect.

Rob Lister, a proponent of this view, argues that there are "certain divine attributes and . . . certain dispositions of passion that God takes on in respect to his creation."[22] These are attributes and states of being that God assumes in addition to his essential attributes for the purpose of relating himself to creatures in time. Lister explains that the distinction between those attributes of being that God doesn't take on—that is, those that belong to his eternal essence—and those that he acquires in drawing near to creatures "fits well with the biblical duality respecting the doctrine of God."[23] It is this same "duality" that he deploys in his attempt to explain God's relation to time.[24]

---

[22] Rob Lister, *God is Impassible and Impassioned: Toward a Theology of Divine Emotion* (Wheaton: Crossway, 2012), 225. These new attributes are not part of God's "intrinsic nature," by which Lister presumably means God's essence, since, as he insists, God's intrinsic nature does not change. See Ibid., 206. Yet they are taken on by God and do really characterize some aspect of his being. This distinction that Lister allows between God's assumed attributes and dispositions and his intrinsic nature probably stems from a rejection of the doctrine of divine simplicity. For Lister, it seems that not all that is in God is ontologically identical with his intrinsic nature or essence.

[23] Lister, *God is Impassible and Impassioned*, 226.

[24] In support of this dualistic understanding of God as timeless and temporal Lister draws on Bruce Ware, *God's Greater Glory: The Exalted God of Scripture and the*

Lister sees a parallel between the widely accepted Christian claim that God is non-spatial in himself and omnipresent in creation, on the one hand, and his claim that God is timeless in himself and omnitemporal in relation to the world, on the other. God is transcendent as timeless and immanent as omnitemporal. Omnitemporality was added to God by virtue of his newly acquired relation to creation and time. Lister draws a distinction between God's "pre-creational timelessness" and his "temporal participation with us, following creation."[25] God's temporality does not displace his essential timelessness, but rather supplements it, so to speak, in order to allow God to create and interact with his creatures in time. Although God's sovereign plan for creation and redemption is eternal, God's "unfolding experience of it occurs in the temporally progressive covenantal context."[26] God does not and, perhaps Lister believes, cannot be present to and act in the world in his eternal essence, but only as the omnitemporal God he has come to be in addition to his timelessness.

John Frame also proposes a dualistic model of divine timelessness and temporality to account for God's relation to the world. On the side of temporality Frame finds the succession of God's work in history to entail that God is temporal in some sense. "The sequence is foreordained by God's decree," he writes, "but he brings it to pass in time."[27] For Frame, the bringing to pass of the decree seems to be a subsequent and different divine act than the decree itself. Moreover, in bringing to pass his sovereign plan God himself enters the vicissitudes of time as covenantally present to it. Frame explains:

> . . . a covenantally present God, like a temporalist God, can know (and assert) temporally indexed expressions like "the sun is rising now." He can feel with human beings the flow of time from one moment to the next. He can react to events in a significant sense. . . .

Christian Faith (Wheaton, IL: Crossway, 2004), 133-39, and John M. Frame, *The Doctrine of God* (Phillipsburg, NJ: P&R Publishing, 2002), 543-59.

[25] Lister, *God is Impassible and Impassioned*, 228-29.

[26] Lister, *God is Impassible and Impassioned*, 230.

[27] Frame, *Doctrine of God*, 558.

> He can mourn one moment and rejoice the next. He can hear and respond to prayer in time. Since God dwells in time, therefore, there is give-and-take between him and human beings. . . . So God is temporal after all, but not merely temporal. He really exists in time, but he also transcends time in such a way as to exist outside it. He is both inside and outside the temporal box—a box that can neither confine him nor keep him out.[28]

How does Frame hold together divine timelessness and temporality? It is tempting to regard his notion of "temporal omnipresence" as a state of being that supplants God's immutability and timelessness, much like Craig maintains. Yet Frame resolutely maintains that "God is unchangeable in his atemporal or supratemporal existence."[29] The key to Frame's doctrine is his apparent belief that God's existence extends beyond his atemporality. As Creator and providential Lord of time, Frame believes that God also exists as a changing being within history itself. In short, "there are two modes of existence in God."[30] Frame does not believe that biblical talk about change in God is merely anthropomorphic, as the classical view explained it. Rather, if God acts in time then he really exists temporally. Frame writes:

> History involves constant change, and so, as an agent in history, God himself changes. On Monday he wants a certain thing to happen, and on Tuesday he wants something else to happen. He is grieved one day and pleased the next. In my view, this is more than just anthropomorphic description. In these accounts, God is not merely *like* an agent in time; he really is *in* time, changing as others change. And we should not say that his atemporal, changeless existence is more real than his changing existence in time, as the term *anthropomorphic* might suggest. Both are real.[31]

Frame is willing to ascribe two existences to God, one timeless and immutable and the other temporal and mutable. The latter is a

---

[28] Frame, *Doctrine of God*, 558-59.
[29] Frame, *Doctrine of God*, 570.
[30] Frame, *Doctrine of God*, 572.
[31] Frame, *Doctrine of God*, 571.

new existential manner of being that Frame believes God assumed at creation. "The difference between God's atemporal and historical existences begins," he explains, "not with the creation of man, but with creation itself."[32] God's act of creating is where Frame locates the origin of his temporality. Yet we are notified that "Neither form of existence contradicts the other."[33] Of course they are ontologically opposite, which is the whole point since God's being as atemporal is not ontologically suited to undergo the temporal changes of being that Frame insists are necessary if God is to meaningfully relate himself to the world.

K. Scott Oliphint proposes a model very similar to Frame's, though he utilizes the hypostatic union of the divine and human natures in Christ as an explanatory key for understanding how God can be both eternal and temporal. Just as the Son is eternal according to his divine nature and temporal according to his human nature, so Oliphint insists that God is eternal in his essential character and temporal in his covenantal character: "he takes on temporal properties without in any way ceasing to be essentially eternal."[34] For Oliphint, as for Frame, the fact of creation and God's action in it is the occasion for attributing new non-essential being to God:

> . . . the fact that God interacts at all with creation presupposes his covenantal character. Once he determines to relate himself to us, that relation entails that he take on properties that he otherwise would not have had. He limits himself while remaining the infinite God. The fact that he is Creator means that he is now related to something *ad extra* to which he was not related before.[35]

On this account, creatorhood is a new, and thus temporal, property in God that is really distinct from what God is as essentially infinite. By "covenantal character" Oliphint indicates a mode of being he

---

32 Frame, *Doctrine of God*, 571.

33 Frame, *Doctrine of God*, 571.

34 K. Scott Oliphint, *God with Us: Divine Condescension and the Attributes of God* (Wheaton: Crossway, 2012), 13, n.8.

35 Oliphint, *God with Us*, 188.

believes God has taken on in addition to his essence in order to interact with creatures. He believes that it is only by assuming the "covenantal property" of temporality that God can create or act in time. The thing that sets Oliphint's view apart from Frame's and Lister's is that he seems to conceive of God's assumed temporality as a creaturely property, given that it is modeled on the Son's assumption of a human nature in the incarnation, rather than a new divine property.[36]

4. Initial evaluation of the various models of divine temporalism

Space does not allow for a thorough evaluation of each temporalist perspective.[37] What should be observed, though, is the common conviction that runs through each of the views presented: *God cannot create or bring about temporal effects without ontologically participating in the temporality of his creation*. Whatever their disagreements may be regarding the notion of divine timelessness—never timeless, no longer timeless, presently timeless and temporal—all divine temporalists are agreed that God must exist temporally in some respect in order to create time and act in history. For God, it takes time to make time and to produce effects in time.

This belief is objectionable on numerous counts. Perhaps most importantly it should be noted that there is an underlying ontological univocism[38] in each of the temporalist models. A temporal effect, the thinking goes, can only proceed from a temporal act of causation and such acts can only go forth from

---

[36] For a critique of Oliphint's notion that God assumes finite properties of being in addition to his essence in order to relate to creation, see James Dolezal, "Objections to K. Scott Oliphint's Covenantal Properties Thesis," *Reformation21*, July 2014, http://www.reformation21.org/articles/objections-to-k-scott-oliphints-covenantal-properties-thesis.php. Accessed 21 January 2015.

[37] For a brief response to the temporalist doctrines from a classical eternalist perspective see Paul Helm's replies to Craig and Wolterstorff in *God and Time: Four Views*, 161-64, 214-18.

[38] By this I mean that God's being is conceived as existing (in some respect) within the same order of being as that of creatures and thus as existentially correlative to them.

temporal agents. Thus, God cannot act in the temporal realm without somehow *existing* on the same temporal ontological continuum with his creatures. Creation, accordingly, is not merely something that goes forth from God, but is also an action that God begins to perform at some point in time. It thereby denotes a real change of activity in him by requiring that he pass from a state of inactivity to activity, of not creating to creating. When God acts to create or produce changes in the world, he himself is moved or changed in the process by becoming the actor he previously was not. Again, for the temporalists this is because God must *be* temporal to just the extent that he acts in and is present to time. Negatively expressed, the basic conviction is that God cannot be present to time in his eternity. Timelessness seems to lock him out of the world; it is a barrier to any action or relation to the world on God's part.

For straight temporalist theologians like Wolterstorff this supposed impediment is reason enough to deny divine timelessness altogether. For the mixed temporalist doctrines, which allow that God was or is timeless in some respect, temporality is needed to supplement the restriction placed on God by his timelessness. Either way God is not able to act in time *as the eternal God*. Moreover, if one accepts that timelessness belongs to God's essence, as the timeless-and-temporal model affirms, then it seems that God cannot act in creation or history according to his divinity, which just is his essence. When God relates himself to creation as both its Creator and Sustainer he is not relating himself to the world *as God*, but as that which he has become in addition to his essential divinity, as the mutable one who changes as others change. This is profoundly inimical to classical Christian orthodoxy as it tends to drive the *divine* agency of God out of the world and to replace it with the presence of a finite and mutable agency.

The consequences of the various temporalist doctrines are catastrophic for the continued confession of classical Christian theism, particularly as it is intended in the various Reformed confessions. To hold any of these versions of temporalism requires the relinquishment of the traditional understanding of a host of doctrines besides God's eternity, including divine infinity, immutability, and simplicity. Is this a price we should be willing to pay? Are there any advantages to upholding the classical eternity doctrine? And what do we make of the challenge of creation? Does not the traditional doctrine entail the strange belief that God is eternally Creator? It is to these questions that we now turn.

Fundamentals of the Classical Eternity Doctrine

Before tackling the question of whether God produces temporal effects as an eternal agent, it is fitting that we survey some of the fundamental features of the classical eternity doctrine in order to appreciate its approach to Scripture and its theological appeal. Also, a few observations will be made concerning the temporalist departures from the doctrine. We will consider: (1) the meaning of divine eternity; (2) the traditional approach to interpreting eternity passages in Scripture; and (3) the dogmatic motivations for the doctrine. This should set the stage for the reaffirmation of God's eternal creatorhood in the final section.

1. Meaning of divine eternity

The basic claim of the classical eternity doctrine is that God does not experience successive states of being and thus has no future and no past. Positively, eternity derives from the belief that God is so perfect and infinite in being that no new state of actuality can come upon him and no state of actuality can slip away from him. He is purely and infinitely actual in all that he is. Boethius memorably describes God's eternity as "the whole, simultaneous and perfect possession of boundless life."[39] A bounded life, by contrast, is one that comes into one's possession little by little and which is also liable to pass out of one's possession. The Boethian formula was reproduced after the sixth century by countless theologians. The Reformed theologian Francis Turretin unfolds its meaning:

---

[39] Boethius, *Philosophiae Consolationis*, V, 6 [10-11], in *The Theological Tractates / The Consolation of Philosophy*, trans. H. F. Stewart, E. K. Rand and S. J. Tester (Cambridge, MA: Harvard University Press, 1973).

> True eternity has been defined by the Scholastics to be "the interminable possession of life—complete, perfect, and at once." Thus it excludes succession no less than end and ought to be conceived as a standing, but not a flowing, now. The reason is because nothing flows away with time from the life of God as from ours. God has every moment at once whatever we have dividedly by succession of time. Hence philosophes have well said that neither the future nor the past (he will be or was), but only the present (he is) can properly be applied to him. For the eternal duration of God embraces indeed all time—the past, present and future; but nothing in him can be past or future because his life remains always the same and immutable.[40]

Geerhardus Vos echoes this same sentiment when he defines eternity as, "That attribute of God whereby He is exalted above all limitations of time and all succession of time, and in a single indivisible present possesses the content of his life perfectly (and as such is the cause of time)."[41]

That which is perfect and indivisible in being cannot be subject to change, mutation, or movement. It cannot acquire or lose any actuality. But all temporal succession involves change from one state of being to another. Turretin thus writes, "[F]or he is not always the same for whom almost every moment something anteriorly is removed and by whom posteriorly something is added." He adds, "The succession and flow of the parts of duration (which exist successively) necessarily involve a certain species of motion (which cannot be applied to God)."[42] Successive duration, or time, is the measure of a thing's movement from state of being *A*

---

[40] Francis Turretin, *Institutes of Elenctic Theology*, ed. James T. Dennison, trans. George Musgrave Giger, vol. 1 (Phillipsburg, NJ: P&R Publishers, 1992), III.10.6.

[41] Geerhardus Vos, *Reformed Dogmatics: Volume 1: Theology Proper*, trans. and ed. Richard B. Gaffin, Jr. (Bellingham, WA: Lexham Press, 2014), 10. This phrasing is reproduced almost verbatim by Louis Berkhof in his *Systematic Theology* (Grand Rapids: William B. Eerdmans Publishing Company, 1996), 60.

[42] Turretin, *Institutes of Elenctic Theology*, III.10.3. It should be clear that when Turretin elsewhere speaks of God's "eternal duration" he is using "duration" in an improper and accommodated sense. Properly understood duration denotes a thing's successive manner of existence.

to state of being *B*. Eternity, then, is the negation of these three ingredients of all temporality: (1) a *terminus ad quo*, (2) a *terminus ad quem*, and (3) the measure of movement between them.[43] Stephen Charnock states, "All other things pass from one state to another; from their original to their eclipse and destruction; but God possesses his being in one indivisible point, having neither beginning, end, nor middle."[44] Edward Leigh defines eternity and time in this same vein:

> Eternity is a being without limitation of time, or a being without beginning, ending, or succession. Time is the continuance of things past, present and to come, all time hath a beginning, a vicissitude, and an end, or may have, but God's essence is bounded by none of these hedges.[45]

Protestant scholastic Benedict Pictet concludes, "In this eternity we cannot conceive of any thing prior or posterior, any thing past, present, or future."[46]

2. Traditional interpretation of eternity passages in Scripture

Many modern theologians find the classical eternity doctrine difficult to harmonize with the language of Scripture. When one

---

[43] This is a standard denial in the classical Christian tradition. Thomas Aquinas expresses this common outlook when he explains, "[E]eternity is known from two sources: first, because what is eternal is interminable—that is, has no beginning nor end (that is, no term either way); secondly, because eternity has no succession, being simultaneously whole." *Summa theologiae* I.10.4, in translation as *Summa Theologica*, trans. Fathers of the English Dominican Province, 5 vols. (Allen, TX: Christian Classics, 1981).

[44] Stephen Charnock, *The Existence and Attributes of God*, 2 vols. (1853; reprint, Grand Rapids: Baker Book House, 1979), 1:284.

[45] Edward Leigh, *A Systeme or Body of Divinity* (London: William Lee, 1662), 176.

[46] Benedict Pictet, *Christian Theology*, trans. Frederick Reyroux (London: R. B. Seeley and W. Burnside, 1834), 98. A "present" is here denied of God in the sense of that temporal moment which stands between the future and the past. In this respect it is not proper to speak of God's "now" or "present" in ordinary temporally indexed fashion. God's actuality is not contained by a present moment relative to a past or future as the "now" of any creature must be.

reads the biblical passages that speak of God's eternity, it is not immediately clear that God is atemporal. Numerous passages speak of eternity in terms agreeable to the notion of an unending succession of moments. Still other passages speak of God as exalted above and before all time, as if he stood beyond its measure. How does the eternalist account for this diversity in maintaining the classical form of the doctrine?

First, Scripture applies the language of eternity in an improper fashion to many things that are not eternal in the strict sense. It speaks, for instance: of an eternal covenant (Gen. 17:7), an eternal possession of land (Gen. 17:8), eternal Mosaic rites, ceremonies, and promises (Num. 10:8; 15:15; 18:8, 11, 19, 23), eternal mountains (Gen. 49:26; Deut. 33:15), of Solomon's temple on Mount Zion as God's eternal dwelling place (1 Kings 8:13; 9:3; Psalm 132:14), of the earth as immovable forever and ever (Psalm 104:5), of eternal life given to God's elect (John 10:28; Titus 1:2), of an eternal weight of glory presently being produced in believers (2 Cor. 4:17), and of an eternal heavenly home awaiting God's people (2 Cor. 5:1). Each of these realities has a temporal beginning and proceeds through a succession of moments. Some have already passed away and will never return. Others will pass away at the end of this present age. Still others will go on endlessly into the future. Turretin observes that eternalist language is used for these various temporal realities

> because on account of their long continuance and constant duration they seem to approach eternity; or it may be used for that which has no end, although it might have had a beginning, as the angels and souls are eternal.[47]

They are more enduring and stable than other temporal things and thus seem to more closely imitate the unchanging eternity of God. Eternity is a comparative term in these instances, denoting those temporal things that are more permanent than others. Inasmuch as God's eternity is an entailment of his absolute immutability,

---

[47] Turretin, *Institutes of Elenctic Theology*, III.10.2. See also, John Gill, *A Body of Divinity* (Grand Rapids: Sovereign Grace Publishers, 1971), 45.

eternalist terms are employed in an imprecise way to describe temporal things that are relatively and comparatively less mutable than other temporal things.

Second, while Scripture uses eternalist terms to describe temporal things, it also employs temporal imagery to speak of God's eternity. He is called the Ancient of Days (Dan. 7:9, 22). It is said that his years have no end (Psalm 102:27). His eternity is said to be "from the day" (Isa. 43:13). He is *before* the created world, *from* everlasting *to* everlasting (Psalm 90:2). Are these expressions to be taken in a strictly literal sense? Is God ancient so as to be thought of as very old? Is his life parceled out by years and days? Is his existence chronologically prior to that of the world and does God advance *from* one state of everlastingness *to* another? The classical interpretation of such expressions regards them as analogies or metaphors meant to accommodate man's inescapable temporal standpoint. Wilhelmus à Brakel explains:

> Even when years or days, or past and present times are attributed to God, and He is called the Ancient of Days and other similar expressions, such is merely done from man's viewpoint. The reason for this is that we, insignificant human beings incapable of thinking and speaking about eternity in a fitting manner, may by way of comparison—comprehend as much of eternity as is needful for us to know. Nevertheless, in doing so we must fully divorce God from the concept of time.[48]

Turretin concurs, stating, "For we who live in time can conceive nothing unless by a relation (*schesin*) to time, in which we are."[49] Girolamo Zanchius says the same: "We being in time cannot understand those things that in God are eternal, but after a manner of things temporal, and such words as signify time."[50] In other

---

[48] Wilhelmus à Brakel, *The Christian's Reasonable Service*, ed. Joel R. Beeke, trans. Bartel Elshout, 4 vols. (Grand Rapids: Reformation Heritage Books, 1992), 1:92.

[49] Turretin, *Institutes of Elenctic Theology*, III.10.14.

[50] Girolamo Zanchius, *Life Everlasting*, ed. Robert Hill (Cambridge: John Legat, 1601), 9. (spelling has been updated) See also, Pictet, *Christian Theology*, 99; and Aquinas, *Summa theologiae* I.10.1, ad 4: "As God, although incorporeal, is named in

words, Scripture accommodates itself to the human manner of speaking and thinking, which is thoroughly temporal.

Third, it is not only the temporal names and adjectives that are given to God that might *prima facie* suggest some temporality in him, but also the unfolding of his effects in time seems to denote temporality in him, namely, the temporality of agency. We rightly speak of a before and after in his works inasmuch as they appear to us successively in time. Yet this also is to be understood from the standpoint of human temporality. In God there is no succession of activity. "When the actions of God are considered as either past or present or future," Turretin maintains, "this is said not with respect to the efficient reason, but in reference to the effects and objects (which are produced in diverse times and on which his acts are terminated)."[51] It seems to be this particular denial of univocal agency that is unacceptable to each of the temporalist positions considered above.

Finally, if the Bible applies eternalist language to temporal things and temporalist terms to the eternal God, then what hope is there for deriving a notion of non-successive eternity from Scripture? In one sense the biblical passages that treat eternity and time *ex professo* tend to underdetermine the question of the precise character of God's eternity. Such elaboration and precision must look to other doctrines for support. Yet there are a few texts that seem to indicate that God is beyond the measure of time altogether inasmuch as they speak of God existing and acting before time: Proverbs 8:22 ("before his works of old"); 2 Timothy 1:9 ("before times eternal"); Titus 1:2 ("before times eternal"), and Jude 25 ("before all time"). Charnock remarks, "[T]o be before all creatures is equivalent to his being from eternity. Time began with the foundation of the world; but God being before time could have no beginning in time."[52] Even so, in order to ensure that eternity is not merely a different sort of successive existence that precedes time—

Scripture metaphorically by corporeal names, so eternity though simultaneously whole, is called by names implying time and succession."

[51] Turretin, *Institutes of Elenctic Theology*, III.10.15.

[52] Charnock, *Existence and Attributes of God*, 1:281.

an uncreated time anterior to created time, so to speak—we must consider the demands of a few other doctrines.

3. Dogmatic motivations for the eternity doctrine

Insisting that the biblical portrayal of God in temporalist terms be understood as analogical and accommodated revelation stems from the conviction that God is infinite, immutable, and simple. These doctrines each prompt the theological conclusion that God's eternity is non-successive in character. We will briefly consider each in turn.

Divine infinity and immensity

Traditionally, many theologians have treated God's eternity under the broader consideration of his infinity.[53] In this respect it has also been construed as a corollary of another aspect of God's infinity, namely, his immensity or omnipresence. Leigh defines infinity as "that whereby God cannot be limited, measured, or determined of anything, being the first cause from whom, and the end whereby all things are made." Thus, God is "free altogether from all limitation of time, place, or degrees."[54] If God is the efficient cause of time he cannot in turn be measured by it. It is customary on this view to regard time as an intrinsic measure of the progress of a thing's being. Bavinck, thus, connects time to finitude:

> [Intrinsic time] is the mode of existence by virtue of which things have a past, present, and future as so many parts which, whatever the standard employed, can be measured and counted. Now whatever can be measured and counted is subject to measure and number and thus limited, for there always remains a measure and a number greater than that which was measured and numbered. Accordingly, the essential nature of time is not that either with

[53] Biblical texts commonly used to establish God's infinity are those that deny limitations to his being or declare him to be immeasurable or unfathomable (e.g., 1 Kings 8:27; Job 11:7-9; Psalm 145:3). Infinity is also built on the understanding of God's perfection as being that to which no higher degree of perfection can be added and thus without limitation.

[54] Leigh, *Systeme or Body of Divinity*, 170.

> respect to the earlier or the later it is finite or endless, but that it encompasses a succession of moments, that there is in it a period that is past, a period that is present, and a period that comes later. But from this it follows that time—intrinsic time—is the mode of existence that is characteristic of all created and finite beings.[55]

A temporal God, even if enduring through an endless succession of moments—as Wolterstorff insists, for example—would still be finite because he would never be complete and perfect in being at any particular moment. His actuality would be comprised of so many temporal parts acquired by him bit by bit, with countless moments ever flowing away from him and countless others ever yet to be actualized in him; but on this understanding he is never actual in the totality of his being at any single moment. This is temporal finitude no matter how endlessly one extends the succession of moments backward and forward.[56]

God's immensity, which is his infinity considered in regard to space, can serve as a helpful parallel in thinking about God's eternity: "for as he is not bounded by space, so neither by time."[57] The doctrine of divine immensity teaches that God in his essence completely fills all places, yet is confined by none. God does not fill space as a body does, that is, he does not fill space spatially or by way of extension.[58] In fine, he does not take on a spatial mode of

---

[55] Bavinck, *Reformed Dogmatics*, 2:162-63. In identifying the essential nature of time as the succession of moments Bavinck seems plainly beholden to Aquinas, *Summa theologiae* I.10.4.

[56] It should be observed that the Christian notion of infinity, in distinction to that of the ancient Greek philosophers, is not conceived as the endless extension of the categories of finite being, but as the transcendence of them altogether. Brakel observes, "We relate to infinity by thinking of a vast expanse. God's infinity, however, excludes the concepts of quantity, dimension, and locality. In order to have any comprehension of the infinity of God's Being, we must, for instance, make a hypothetical comparison to a vast expanse while simultaneously denying such to be characteristic of God." *Reasonable Service*, 1:93. See also, Richard A. Muller, *Post-Reformation Reformed Dogmatics: The Rise and Development of Reformed Orthodoxy, ca. 1520-1725*, 4 vols. (Grand Rapids: Baker Academic, 2003), 3:330.

[57] Gill, *Body of Divinity*, 45.

[58] Turretin explains that Scripture uses the language of God *filling* heaven and earth (Jer. 23:24) in an improper manner inasmuch as filling is itself a spatial term

existence or attributes of extension in order to fill space with his presence. He is present to the world in his essence as the infinite God who upholds it in being by his power. On this classical understanding it follows that omnipresence does not entail omni-spatiality or omni-extensionality. By the same token it would seem that God's presence to all times does not necessitate "omnitemporality" as Lister has it or "temporal omnipresence" as Frame expresses it. Just as God is not spatial in his presence to space so he is not temporal in his presence to time.[59]

Divine immutability

Aquinas notes the inextricable connection between divine immutability and eternity: "The idea of eternity follows immutability, as the idea of time follows movement. . . . Hence, as God is supremely immutable, it supremely belongs to Him to be eternal."[60] Wilhelmus à Brakel echoes this conviction: "God unchangeably exists while time is in progression."[61] If time is indeed the numbering of change or motion, then it should be clear why an immutable God cannot be temporal. He cannot undergo change from an anterior state of being to a subsequent state of being as that would both remove and add actuality to his existence (even if not to his essence as modern day temporalists are keen to remind us). Some temporalists, such as Wolterstorff, are willing to deny the classical doctrine of God's ontological immutability as plainly incompatible with divine temporality. Mixed temporalist views, such as those put forth by Lister and Frame, wish to distinguish between God's immutable essence and his newly assumed mutability of relations and activity with respect to creation. It seems, though, that their position is not really so different than

---

denoting extension: "we have no proper and accurate terms for explaining the ubiquity of God and are compelled here to use phrases borrowed from finite and corporeal things." *Institutes of Elenctic Theology*, III.9.5.

59 For a fine philosophical elaboration of the argument for divine timelessness from divine spacelessness see Paul Helm, *Eternal God: A Study of God without Time*, second ed. (Oxford: Oxford University Press, 2010), 41-55.

60 Aquinas, *Summa theologiae* I.10.2.

61 Brakel, *Reasonable Service*, 1:92. John Gill observes that eternity and immutability "infer one another." *Body of Divinity*, 48.

Wolterstorff's. After all, he too denies that God undergoes essential changes.

A few remarks are here in order regarding the notion of essential change in God. Ontic change need not denote a change in essence. In fact, it is not clear what "essential change" even means unless, perhaps, it is an improper way of describing the creation *ex nihilo* or the annihilation of some entity. Yet many temporalists apparently think it is somehow significant to maintain that God's essence does not change while affirming that he changes in non-essential ways. Properly speaking, not even creaturely essences undergo change. No human, for example, ever existed as essentially non-human, neither will he or she ever be changed from human into non-human. The same rule holds for all other creaturely essences. Change, rather, is located in the loss or acquisition of a particular substance's accidental properties or in the underlying prime matter that perdures through the corruption of one material substantial form and acquisition of another. *Change is not located in essences as such.* Affirming that God is essentially unchanging yet changes in non-essential ways is a fairly unimpressive argument that could equally apply to any creature. It certainly falls short of the intention of the classical immutability doctrine which is only meaningful insofar as it proscribes *all* ontic change to God. When older scholastic theologians denied God's essence undergoes change they intended thereby to deny *all* change in him since, following their commitment to God's simplicity, there could be nothing in God's existence that fell outside his essence. They certainly did not mean that God could change in those non-essential aspects of his being since they flatly rejected the notion that there could possibly be any such aspects. This brings us to a consideration of God's simplicity.

Divine simplicity

Eternity follows from the doctrine of divine simplicity and its denial that God is composed of parts.[62] If God were in time then the

---

[62] This doctrine is rooted in the biblical teaching regarding God's self-sufficiency (e.g., Acts 17:24-25; Rom. 11:35-36). If God is wholly self-sufficient and

full actuality of his life would be built up out of temporal parts, that is, of really distinct before and after moments. Temporal beings must necessarily exhibit a variety of existential states since time is the measure of movement between these states. But if God possesses his life in one indivisible present, as the eternity doctrine insists, then it cannot be a life composed of temporal parts since that which is composed of parts is divisible. For this reason Brakel observes, "There can be no chronology within the Being of God since his Being is simple and immutable."[63] Plainly put, in a simple God there can be no real distinction between before and after and so no temporality, no meditating movement between anterior and posterior states of being. It is no wonder that Brakel, following the implications of simplicity, insists, "God's being is eternity and eternity is God's being."[64]

Modern temporalist theologians are divided on how to respond to the challenge of simplicity. Those of the straight temporal and timeless-turned-temporal persuasions are generally agreed that divine simplicity is an impossible perfection and that Christians are wise to reject it. The dualists of the timeless-and-temporal school tend to be less willing to repudiate the simplicity doctrine. Yet their dualistic model seems to require them to do so inasmuch as it assumes that God's existence extends beyond his essential eternity to encompass also a non-essential temporality. Yet if such were the case there must be a real distinction in God between essence and existence since they are not coextensive. This undercuts the core claim of divine simplicity—that in God existence and essence are identical. It is perhaps possible to avoid this implication if one proceeds as Frame does to speak of two *existences* of God. But the theological outlay of such a move seems too costly. It casts monotheism itself into doubt and raises questions about the unity

---

independent in being then he cannot be composed of parts since that which is so composed depends upon its parts for the various aspects of its being. An independent God must therefore be simple. On simplicity and eternity see James E. Dolezal, *God without Parts: Divine Simplicity and the Metaphysics of God's Absoluteness* (Eugene, OR: Pickwick Publications, 2011), 88-92.

[63] Brakel, *Reasonable Service*, 1:92. Cf. Gill, *Body of Divinity*, 48.

[64] Brakel, *Reasonable Service*, 1:92.

of God's being. Does God have one act of being or two? And if he has two, as Frame's language implies, then how is it that we are not referring to two beings, two Gods? Certainly Frame would not endorse such unorthodox outcomes, though it is not clear how his notion of two divine existences can consistently steer clear of these implications. In the final analysis, the timeless-and-temporal conflict with simplicity appears unavoidable.

Having surveyed these basic components and motives of the traditional doctrine, we are now ready to explore the implications for God's creatorhood.

Creation and Divine Eternity

Did God become Creator? Did he transition from a state of not being Creator to a state of being Creator? According to the temporalist perspective he did. Even those of the mixed timeless-and-temporal persuasion believe that the property of creatorhood falls on the temporal side of God's supposed duality. Oliphint, for instance, writes, "He remains who he is, but he decides to be something else as well; he decides to be the God of the covenant."[65] Oliphint understands Creator to be part of the covenantal "something else" God begins to be.[66] This reality for God is new, he claims, something "which had not been the case before."[67] Plainly, for temporalists God is not an eternal Creator and does not create *as the Eternal One*, which is to say, in virtue of his eternity.[68] Moreover,

---

[65] Oliphint, *God with Us*, 254.

[66] Oliphint, *God with Us*, 16-17.

[67] Oliphint, *God with Us*, 255. Oliphint appears to believe that creatorhood is not a *divine* reality since he is clear that this is a property assumed by God in addition to his essence (which simply is his divinity). The fact that he founds this explanation on an incarnational model of the Son's assumption of a human nature strongly suggests the peculiar notion that God's creatorhood is not divine just as the Son's assumed humanity is not divine.

[68] Note that properties are commonly understood as ontological foundations for action, those features of a thing's being in virtue of which it acts. For example, a wise man acts wisely in virtue of the wisdom that is in him, and a strong man performs feats of strength in virtue of the property of power in him, and so forth. With respect to God's action we might similarly say that God acts in virtue of what

it seems fair to conclude that for all temporalists, including those who wish to retain some affirmation of essential eternality in God, God does not possess the content of his life perfectly in one indivisible now and neither does he remain always the same in the totality of his being.

Eternalists disagree and have traditionally been quite willing to endorse the incomprehensible notion that God is immutably and eternally Creator. Vos, after affirming God's successionless eternality, states that God "*as such* is the cause of time" (see above). That is to say that God's eternity requires no augmentation, no acquisition of some temporality, in order to create time. His eternity *itself* posits time and causes all temporal things to be. God's action in establishing and upholding time is not founded on some temporal feature of his being, but on his eternal and infinite essence. It is for this reason Bavinck affirms that God directly acts in the world in virtue of his essence, denying that he needs intermediary (i.e., non-essential) properties of being to act in the created order:

> [I]t is God who posits the creature, eternity which posits time, immensity which posits space, being which posits becoming, immutability which posits change. *There is nothing intermediate between these two classes of categories*: a deep chasm separates God's being from that of all creatures.[69]

God's agency in and toward creation cannot be divorced from his being or accounted for in terms of something that he has become in addition to what he is essentially. In order to grasp this it is first important to note the distinction between the manner in which we

---

is in him. Thus, if creatorhood is not in God eternally then it must be that he does not act in creation *as eternal*, that is, in virtue of his eternality. He must acquire some property of being in addition to his eternal essence in order to act in the world. This is similar, perhaps, to the way a wise man, who is not wise in virtue of his human essence, must acquire wisdom in addition to his essence in order to act wisely. For those who deny that creatorhood belongs to God in his eternal essence it must follow that God does not act in the world in virtue of his divine essence, but rather in virtue of that which he has come to be in addition to that essence.

[69] Bavinck, *Reformed Dogmatics*, 2:158-59. Emphasis added.

predicate the name Creator of God and the manner in which this reality is in him ontologically.

1. Creator as a relative name denoting an absolute reality

God comes to be known and named by us as Creator through our observation of his created effects in time. But in identifying this relation we are not picking out a newly acquired property of being in God. Zanchius observes:

> Those names which argue a relative respect between God and his creatures, as the names Creator, Lord, Redeemer, [and so forth] are indeed in time given to him, and not from eternity, yet so as that no new thing is added to him, neither is there any change in him.[70]

Creator, Lord, and Redeemer are not accidental features of existence that are appended to God's essence. Bavinck writes similarly, "Relative names, such as 'Lord,' 'Creator,' 'Sustainer,' 'Savior' and so on, belong to God only on account of and upon the coming into being of, the creation."[71] Yet he further explains that all the names assumed by God in virtue of the various ways he relates himself to creatures "definitively denote something in God that exists in him absolutely . . ."[72] Many Reformed theologians point to Augustine's remarks along these same lines:

> Accordingly, that which is first said of God in time, and was not said of him before, is manifestly said of him relatively, yet not because of some accident in God, as though something happened to him, but plainly on account of some accident of that with reference to which God begins to be called something relative.[73]

---

70 Zanchius, *Life Everlasting*, 20 (spelling updated).
71 Bavinck, *Reformed Dogmatics*, 2:133-34.
72 Bavinck, *Reformed Dogmatics*, 2:134.
73 Augustine, *De Trinitate*, V, 16, cited in Bavinck, *Reformed Dogmatics*, 2:134.

It is not difficult to stumble on Augustine's and Bavinck's twofold affirmation in this connection. On the one hand they insist that God is not called Creator from eternity and on the other maintain that this name, Creator, picks out an absolute reality in God and is not something he began to be. What are we to make of this? It is perhaps helpful to understand the difference between the twin affirmations—Creator is a relative name and denotes an absolute reality—as corresponding to the epistemic/noetic activity of the human knower, on the one hand, and ontological reality of God's absolute being, on the other. The difference, then, lies not in a twofold manner of God's existence—timeless and temporal, say—but in the distinction between the human manner of knowing and predicating about God and God's manner of existing. The coming-to-be and the relativity, so to speak, are in the event and manner of humans naming God as Creator, but not in the being and activity of God.

2. Creation as an eternal act producing a temporal effect

If creation and time began to be, then must it not follow that God's act of creating also began to be? Temporalists believe that an affirmative answer is the only possibility. Eternalists do not. Perhaps the deepest difference between these two approaches is that the former generally presupposes a univocal account of God's agency, such that all causes are ontologically correlative to their effects, which includes ontic correlativity upon the timeline in which the effects exist. Thus, God must be a temporal actor when he produces temporal beings and events. Eternalists deny this univocal account of divine agency.

Specifically, they deny that the intrinsic divine act by which God creates is temporal. In fact, the divine act of creation is none other than the eternal act of God's immutable will. If God's will for the world is eternal then so is his effective agency as Creator, since his will to create the world simply is his act of creating. He does not need to supplement his eternal will with any additional action or agency. We may contrast this, for example, to human productions in which the act of producing follows after and is really distinct from the act of planning to produce, as driving the nails is a distinct and subsequent act to drawing up the blueprints. In God there is no such distinction since the purposing (the willing) is the doing. Turretin explains that when the world goes forth from God into being "No new will enters into him, but only a new external work proceeds from his eternal efficacious and omnipotent will." He further states, "By the same practical volition which he had from eternity, he created the world in time—produced it actually in the beginning of time."[74] The divine act of production is not what begins with time, but only the thing produced. As the eternal will to produce is efficacious and powerful, it requires no subsequent and distinct act of agency and thus no temporality in God.

The question of eternal creation can be needlessly complicated if we fail to distinguish between the senses in which the term "creation" is used. It can be employed verbally to describe God's act of creating or it can be used nominally to describe the things created, the world and all that is in it. The former is eternal and the latter is not. Leigh observes that some acts of God proceed from his being and terminate upon creatures. When we speak of these acts—such as creation, providence, vocation, sanctification, and glorification—we need to distinguish between the act itself in God and the things upon which that act terminates, as Leigh insists:

> . . . we must distinguish between the action itself, and the work. God's act in Creating is the act of his will, that such a Creature should stand up in time, *Creatio* is but *Essentia Divinis relationae ad Creaturam*, Aquinas. But if we consider *opus*, the work itselfe, so the Creatures have a being one after another.[75]

Creation is an eternal act that produces a temporal result.[76] This distinction between *actus*, as the eternal divine act of creating, and

[74] Turretin, *Institutes of Elenctic Theology*, III.7.1.

[75] Leigh, *Systeme or Body of Divinity*, 177-78. The reference to Aquinas is drawn from *Summa theologiae* I.45.3, ad 1: "Creation signified actively means the divine action, which is God's essence, with a relation to the creature."

[76] This is not to suggest that the world is temporal because it chronologically follows after some period of duration that preceded it. The world's absolute

opus, as the temporal work created, is absolutely crucial if we are to maintain a sufficiently strong Creator/creature distinction and resist the temptation to temporalize God in order to explain his acts of agency. It is in obscuring this distinction that theologians are moved to introduce temporality into God.

3. Eternal Creator

If God's act of creation is eternal then he is the eternal Creator of time. It won't do to insist that this cannot be because all agents are temporally correlative to their effects. Such reasoning merely begs the question by assuming that all acts of agency must conform univocally to the manner of finite creaturely agency. Why can't God *as* eternal and *as* immutable bring about temporal beings and changing events? Why must he ontologically assume temporality in order to create and act in his temporal creation? On the contrary, the more important question may be: How could a temporal and changing God possibly be the ultimate cause and explanation of time and change? All that changes ultimately requires an unchanging foundation for its being. It seems that only an agent acting *as eternal and immutable* is sufficient enough in being to posit all time and change. Only an eternal Creator can create time.

Bavinck maintains this mystery in a striking passage:

> On the one hand it is certain that God is the Eternal One: in him there is neither past or future, neither becoming or change. All that he is is eternal: his thought, his will, his decree. Eternal in him is the idea of the world that he thinks and utters in the Son; eternal in him is also the decision to create the world; eternal in him is the will that created the world in time; eternal is also the act of

---

beginning in existence is not a moment that succeeds a previous moment. Such an understanding would effectively deny that time begins with creation since the period that precedes creation would be temporally proximate to the world as its chronological predecessor. The world, understood as the totality of the created order, does not chronologically follow or precede anything. Rather all succession between before and after is within the world itself. Strictly speaking, creation appears *with* time, not *in* time. See Augustine, *Confessions*, bk. XI, chs. 10-13; and Bavinck, *RD*, II: 429: "the world was not made in time but along with time."

> creating as an act of God, an action both internal and immanent. For God did not *become* Creator, so that first for a long time he did not create and then afterward he did create. Rather he is the eternal Creator, and as Creator he was the Eternal One, and as the Eternal One he created. The creation therefore brought about no change in God.[77]

If such an understanding is correct then it effectively eliminates one of the leading motives for maintaining a temporalist doctrine of God. God does not need to be (or become) like his temporal creation in order to create it or to act within it.

Conclusion

Maintaining the classical eternity doctrine undoubtedly requires one to confess a deep and inscrutable mystery. In affirming that God is eternal Creator we may readily say with John Owen that we cannot think what we have confessed, but we do adore. To remove or mollify this mystery by the introduction of temporality into God ultimately has deleterious consequences for our ability to confess consistently divine eternity and to worship God as eternal. It is to suggest that God does not act in the world as the God that he is from all eternity, but as something finite that he has come to be. If God acts in the world as the Creator he has *become,* as each of the temporalist paradigms assumes, then we do not adore him *as divine* when we worship him as Creator. Only the *eternal* Creator is worthy of our highest reverence, worship, and obedience.[78]

---

[77] Bavinck, *Reformed Dogmatics*, 2:429. Emphasis his.

[78] I am grateful to Paul Helm for his helpful remarks on an earlier draft of this article.

BOOK REVIEWS

Divine Covenants and Moral Order: A Biblical Theology of Natural Law,

David VanDrunen
(Grand Rapids: W. B. Eerdmans Publishing Co., 2014, 545 pp.),
reviewed by Micah Renihan

In 2010 David VanDrunen published his first major work on natural law entitled *Natural Law and the Two Kingdoms*. He has followed up that work with another examination of natural law in *Divine Covenants and Moral Order*. While the first book focused upon the place of natural law and two kingdoms theology in the history of the theology of the church, this present volume approaches the topic from the perspective of Scripture. VanDrunen seeks to show that Scripture itself presents a robust theology of natural law. In particular, the covenants God makes with man provide the framework for understanding natural law.

The book consists of two parts. In part 1 VanDrunen elaborates on the relationship between covenant and natural law as seen in the created order and with reference to the entire human race. Chapter 1 argues that in the very act of creation God set man in the context of natural law by way of the *imago Dei* and the covenant of creation (or covenant of works). As such, man was bestowed with a "protological image" in which Adam was to image God's pattern of working and achieving rest (41, 72-73). This protological image required that man act with "creative and loving fruitfulness" and "pursue proportionate retributive justice" (without mercy) as he sought to fulfill the creation mandate (91-93).

Chapter 2 could be considered the most important chapter for VanDrunen's thesis. In it he argues that, because sin made it impossible for man to fulfill the requirements of the protological image, it was necessary for God to reissue the creation mandate in a refracted form. In the Noahic covenant "God preserves (but does not redeem) the world and maintains human beings in his image, and thereby continues to promulgate natural law" (96). The Noahic covenant becomes the lens through which the original covenant requirements to Adam are refracted upon the entire human race. But it does so at a penultimate level. It does not save man from his predicament; it simply preserves him in the midst of it. This leads VanDrunen to say that "(common)-grace-preserves-nature and (saving)-grace-consummates-nature" (98). The common grace shown in the Noahic covenant establishes the basis by which humanity may be preserved. Thus it gives to us a "bare minimalist ethic concerning intrahuman affairs" (123). The requirements of this ethic include proper eating, proper procreation, and proportionate retributive justice that is tempered by forbearance. VanDrunen argues that this ethic may be expanded as wisdom is used to apply it to different situations.

Some of the most interesting material in the book, for me, came in chapters 3-4, which describe the ways that Scripture demonstrates this ethic as being present in the Gentile nations around Israel. It is seen in the condemnation of Sodom, in Abraham's dealings with Abimelech, and in the rebukes to the nations by Israel's prophets (as VanDrunen points out, the prophets never rebuke the nations for failing to keep the Mosaic law per se, but for violations of the natural law). In the final chapter of part 1, VanDrunen explores the way that Paul condemns the Gentiles in Romans 1:18-2:16 on the basis of what they knew of their responsibilities before God as they understood it from the created order and apart from the Mosaic law.

Having examined the foundations of natural law in the created order, especially as refracted through the Noahic covenant, VanDrunen turns to consider the teaching of Scripture on the relationship between the covenant of grace and natural law in part 2. Chapter 6 is a discussion of the Abrahamic covenant. VanDrunen argues that while the Abrahamic covenant provides an eschatological moral standard (that is, an ethic for those in the covenant of grace and destined for eternal life), it does not nullify natural law. Instead, it provides the framework by which Abraham could understand God's justice, and it gives Abraham a basis by which he could interact with the rest of the world.

The difficult (and controversial) topic of the Mosaic law is dealt with in chapter 7. The Mosaic law, he argues, has both protological and eschatological (redemptive) elements to it, though he primarily focuses on the protological aspect. From this perspective, the Mosaic covenant is seen as a republication of the covenant of creation insofar as it also operates by the principle "do this and live." VanDrunen ably argues that the Mosaic law is one particular application of the natural law to a particular society in its particular circumstances. Thus it provides an example to be learned from (though not necessarily copied) in the application of natural law. This chapter includes an examination of several portions of the Torah as well as numerous reflections from the New Testament on the connection between the Mosaic law and natural law.

Another fascinating portion of the book is the discussion in chapter 8 of natural law and the wisdom literature. With a focus on the book of Proverbs, VanDrunen demonstrates a remarkable level of similarity between the wisdom displayed in the proverbs and the basic requirements of the natural law. Instructions regarding sexual purity, an honest work ethic, and proportionate justice may be found all throughout the book of Proverbs. What is of special note is the way that Proverbs draws upon the natural order to make many of its observations. In addition, it may be argued that some of the individual proverbs actually have their origins in the Gentile nations.

The final chapter provides something of a framework for how Christians ought to consider their relationship to natural law. VanDrunen argues that we are still bound by the natural law, but in a penultimate way. The protological natural law requirement as set out in the covenant of creation has been fulfilled by Christ and thus the burden of fulfilling that law in order to attain eschatological rest no longer binds us. However, the Noahic refraction of the natural law is still binding upon us (as is the moral law which is broader than natural law and stands throughout all of the covenants), especially as it enables us to interact with unbelievers. However, as those who are in the middle of the already and the not-yet of eschatological consummation, we find ourselves under a dual ethic with respect to natural law. We are not only bound by the refracted

Noahic law, but also by the new ethic introduced by Jesus Christ for the new creation. In this ethic there is an emphasis upon showing mercy and grace because we have been the recipients of that same mercy and grace. Since Christ has already paid the penalty for our sins, we no longer need to pursue proportionate retributive justice in the church. Instead, we show forgiveness and even receive further hurt at times. Just as our Savior endured wrongs done against him, so also should his disciples. "Human beings, as it were, slapped God in the face through their sin, and God responded with the *lex talionis* - not by justly slapping them back but by bearing that retaliatory slap himself through Jesus" (458).

The book ends with a conclusion that reviews the argument of the book and suggests some basic ways in which Christians may use natural law in the public arena. Three areas he addresses are 1) support for natural institutions, 2) a view of justice that incorporates retribution and restoration, and 3) the place of religious liberty. The book also includes five appendices on various topics.

VanDrunen has done an excellent job in this volume of making his case from Scripture. With his usual clarity and precision he identifies and addresses the key issues and key texts. He interacts with a number of very difficult passages but does so in a balanced way. The result is a book that is very helpful for both theology and practice.

Two reservations may be noted regarding the book. First, VanDrunen's understanding of the covenant of grace is the usual paedobaptist view of including the Abrahamic covenant as an administration of the covenant of grace. As a Baptist, I disagree with this analysis. However, it does not change his argument substantially. Understanding the Abrahmic covenant as typological of the covenant of grace allows for the same basic analysis of the various texts surveyed. A second reservation about the book regards those who were saved prior to Christ's incarnation. Before Christ came, the protological natural law requirement given in the covenant of creation had not been fulfilled, so would that not necessitate that believers in the Old Testament were still under that requirement to fulfill the creation mandate as given to Adam? It is clear that New Testament believers may live with the knowledge that Christ has fulfilled the creation mandate for them, but it is not clear that Old Testament believers could have had the same perspective. Nevertheless, these reservations are quite minor and should not deter anyone from reading such a valuable and helpful book.

God with Us: Divine Condescension and the Attributes of God

K. Scott Oliphint
(Wheaton, IL: Crossway Books, 2012, 302pp.),
reviewed by Charles J. Rennie

Our contemporary theological context has witnessed much debate about the relationship between God's transcendence and immanence, or his absolute and relative attributes. Within the last century, theological questions have been raised that have set the agenda of the debate as theologians continue to seek adequate solutions to how we understand God in relation to the world. What underlies much of the debate is the presupposition that transcendence and immanence are opposing concepts, such that transcendence is viewed as a problem that needs to be overcome for God's immanence to be possible. How can the wholly transcendent and independent being of classical theism personally and sincerely relate and respond to creation, much less create at all, without jeopardizing his otherness? Moreover, which biblical texts should be given the priority for an understanding of who or what God is, those which emphasize God's independence and immutability or those which imply a degree of dependence upon the creature (i.e., God's grieving, repenting, etc.)? While open theists have consistently given priority to God's immanence over his transcendence, it is suggested by Dr. K. Scott Oliphint that classical theism has not taken God's condescension, which is expressed by way of covenant, seriously enough (14).

In *God with Us*, K. Scott Oliphint declares both of the above solutions inadequate and therefore proposes a new way of understanding God-in-relation that is "compatible" with God-in-himself. His thesis is that although God is transcendent and altogether independent, he nonetheless freely "takes on characteristics that determine just how he will interact with us, and with creation generally" (12). Central to his thesis is the concern to interpret fully and literally those passages of Scripture that describe God-in-relation, by way of voluntary condescension, without jeopardizing his independence. Citing the WCF 7.1, "The distance between God and the creature is so great . . .", he proposes that God has voluntarily condescended to us by way of covenant by taking on certain properties that enable him to relate to us in a way that we may know him. He variously refers to these "characteristics" that God "takes on" as created and temporal properties (13, n. 8, 120, 198, 208, 209), non-essential properties (16), and covenantal properties (40). Oliphint proposes that God "takes on" these created properties in a manner analogous to the divine Son's assumption of created properties in the incarnation, without altering his *essential* properties and necessary attributes. When God asked Adam and Eve in the garden, "Where are you?" Oliphint explains, "In condescending to relate to Adam and Eve, he is, like them (not essentially, but covenantally), restricted in his knowledge of where they might be hiding in that garden" (111). Or again, after rejecting the distinction between literal and anthropomorphic locutions, he writes:

> When Scripture says that God changes his mind, or that he is moved, or angered by our behavior, we should see that as literal. It refers us to God and to his dealings with us. It is as literal or as real as God being the God of Abraham, Isaac, and Jacob. But we should also see that the God who really changes his mind is the accommodated God, the *yarad-cum*-Emmanuel God who, while remaining the "I Am," nevertheless stoops to our level to interact, person-to-person, with us. His change of mind does not effect his essential character, any more than Christ dying on the cross precluded him from being fully God. He remains fully and completely God, a God who is not like man that he should change

> his mind, and he remains fully and completely the God who, in covenant with us, changes his mind to accomplish his sovereign purposes. (123-24)

Thus, when God takes on the covenantal properties of grief and sorrow and ignorance, he really and literally grieves and sorrows and acquires knowledge by virtue of those properties, though he remains independent and *essentially* unchanged. In this manner, Oliphint seeks to take God's voluntary condescension seriously, while simultaneously affirming the immutability of God's necessary and essential attributes.

In the Introduction, Oliphint outlines the theological method he attempts to apply throughout. Intent on resisting a transcendence versus immanence approach, he advocates what he calls

> a biblical notion of compatibility (affirmed in christology) [that] can provide a context in which we can take God's activity in relation to us and creation seriously while at the same time affirming the Reformed understanding of God's aseity. (44)

Citing the WCF 1.9, Oliphint (in opposition to Peter Enns' *Inspiration and Incarnation*) affirms that, because the Bible has a single divine author, Scripture must be interpreted by Scripture, the more obscure texts interpreted in light of those places that speak more clearly and in a manner consistent with the scope of the whole, which is the glory of God. In this way systematic theology and the unity of Scripture are given a critical role in determining the legitimate exegetical conclusions of any given text. Quoting Moisés Silva, Oliphint confesses that our "theological system should tell [us] how to exegete" (25). With the Westminster "system of doctrine" in mind, he affirms that the priority must be given to those passages that speak of God's absolute independence, what he is in himself before anything existed outside himself. "Those passages are clearer because they articulate the 'divine nature' of God; they tell us something of who he essentially is" (29). Such a priority is not intended to neglect those passages which describe God-in-relation to his creation, but to emphasize that such descriptions of God must be interpreted in a manner "compatible" with his absolute independence.

> Passages that speak of God being sorry or ignorant of historical events or of our own commitment to him automatically demand questions. They cry out for resolution because we know enough about God's 'Godness' (θειότης—Rom. 1:20) to know that he cannot be both independent and dependent in the same way. Yet there are passages that clearly note some level of dependence. . . . [e.g.,] We rightly question how such regret coheres with God's independence. (29)

To Oliphint's credit, he offers a biblical and classical defense of God's aseity in chapter one, as well as several divine attributes that may necessarily be deduced from it (i.e., divine simplicity, infinity, and immutability). However, his precise proposal of "compatibility" and "covenantal properties" (chapter 2), which he believes is affirmed in christology (chapters 3 and 4), is both novel and nebulous to say the least. The reader, particularly the one whose theological system informs his theological conclusions as Oliphint has suggested, may anticipate being left with several questions in search of coherency.

The most basic question is, "What are these so-called covenantal properties?" This question is essential to his proposal, and yet it is a concept which is never clearly defined. Perhaps, in part, this is because Oliphint assumes that it is

> intuitive enough that most would see immediately what we generally mean . . . that God freely determined to take on attributes, characteristics, and properties that he did not have, and would not have, without creation. (110)

One could wish he would have relied less upon intuition and more upon definition. What is clear is that it is a concept which is proposed in order to explain God's condescension, whether it be in the form of theophany, anthropomorphism, or the relative attributes in general.

Oliphint attempts to establish the necessity and legitimacy of the concept of covenantal properties with regard to God's relative attributes in general. He repeatedly uses the example of "Creator," and asks whether it is of the essence of God. Because Creator is predicated of God *relative to creation*, Oliphint argues that it cannot be an essential property of God. Otherwise it would have been necessary for God to create, for it is argued that God cannot be considered Creator apart from creation. Therefore he concludes, "It would seem, then, that God has properties that are essential to him and others that are not essential to him" (17). God "takes on" these so-called covenantal properties, in addition to his essential properties, in order to condescend in creating and relating to his creation.

However, Oliphint's argument assumes what it fails to prove, that the so-called relative attributes of classical theism are called such because they are ontologically relative in God. The novelty of this assumption needs to be pointed out. Zanchi, for instance, addresses the question very differently. He writes:

> [H]e cannot be changed . . . by any passive potency which is in himself. For he is a most simple and perfect act; and therefore cannot be in potency to anything, be it essential, or accidental. All other things may be changed by his power, by which they are, and upon which they depend. (*Life Everlasting*, 73)

God possesses an uncreated active potency, that is, a power to create which belongs only to a Creator, whether he chose to create or not. God's power is a from-eternity-active power. In other words, God is pure *act,* all-potent, an ever-living, always active agent with the active potency to effect change outside of himself, without any passive potency whatsoever to undergo change within himself. Thus, Zanchi concludes:

> Those names which argue a relative respect betwixt God and his creatures, and the names Creator, Lord, Redeemer, &c. are indeed in time given to him, and not from eternity, yet so as that no new thing is added to him, neither is there any change in him. (*Life Everlasting,* 20)

The name Creator signifies an absolute *reality* belonging to God from eternity. Yet, it is a *name* which is given to him relatively by us, in so far as it signifies a new relation established *in the creature* relative to the ever-existing immutable Creator. Unlike the relative attributes of classical theism, Oliphint's newly proposed covenantal properties are non-essential, ontologically relative, created realities in God that are assumed to be necessary, not only for God to be able to create, but also for him to be capable of relating to his creation.

Moreover, Oliphint maintains that this notion of covenantal properties is "affirmed in christology." The incarnation is the quintessential example of God's condescension. In the incarnation, the eternal, divine Son of God took on a human nature without ceasing to be what he essentially was. It was not the union or confusion of two natures, but the assumption of a human nature by the second person of the Trinity. One person with two natures, that is, with created covenantal properties and essential properties, without confusion, change, division, or separation. According to Oliphint, Christology provides the paradigm for theology and for our understanding of all forms of divine condescension. Just as God the Son took on human covenantal properties without changing what he essentially was, so also God has taken on created covenantal properties from the foundation of the world without changing what he essentially is. Oliphint uses the Reformed *communicatio idiomatum,* that the properties of each nature of Christ may be communicated to the person, to explain how God can be said to repent, grieve, and so on, without ceasing to be the eternal, immutable, and independent God. For example, just as the Scripture states that the Son grew in wisdom, according to his human nature, without implying any change of wisdom in his divine nature, so it may be really and truly said that God, according to his covenantal properties, repents without implying any change in his divine essence. In short, God has taken on created properties from the foundation of the world in the same way that the Son of God took on created human properties in the incarnation. "What is true of the incarnation is true also of other 'incarnations' of God in Scripture" (192). Therefore, covenantal properties are created "incarnational" properties and attributes that God really and truly takes on prior to the incarnation in order for him to relate to that which is not himself.

Such a proposal raises several unhappy consequences. For instance, are we to apply the concept to each person of the Trinity, or just the Son? On the one hand, if it is consistently applied to each, we must conclude one of two things.[1] Either we are to conceive of these properties accidentally, and therefore reject divine simplicity, or they are to be conceived of substantially. Oliphint appears to prefer the latter, arguing that in the incarnation the Son of God did not merely take on accidental properties but rather assumed a substantial union of two natures in one person (152-54). If this is so, then we are led to the unfortunate conclusion that all three persons have had two substantial natures, one created and one divine, from the foundation of the world. It would seem difficult, therefore, to escape the conclusion that all three persons, to a greater or lesser extent, have been incarnate at one point or another.

On the other hand, it could be argued that Oliphint's emphasis appears to limit the concept to the person of the Son. And yet, doing so would fail to take into account *all* of the relative and anthropomorphic language of Scripture. According to his proposal, in order for Israel to really and truly "grieve His Holy Spirit" (Isa. 63:10), the person of the Spirit would also have to take on created covenantal properties. Likewise, are we to assume that only the second person of the Trinity took on the property of Creator? As an aside, it must also be concluded, contrary to Oliphint's insistence (186), that God would have to assume these pre-incarnate properties permanently, otherwise the Father would cease to be Creator and the Spirit could not be said to be capable of grief in the Old and New Testaments alike (cf. Eph. 4:30). Therefore, in order for his proposal to accomplish what he intends, it must apply equally and personally to each person of the Trinity, both in the New Testament as well as the Old—an untenable position indeed!

---

[1] It is altogether unclear whether Oliphint is arguing for a third option, and it is equally unclear what that could be.

However, assuming for sake of argument that the concept may coherently be applied exclusively to the Son, the redemptive-historical consequences are no less concerning. It seems that Oliphint's desire is to interpret every relative attribute of God, theophany, and anthropomorphism as the Son of God's pre-incarnate incarnated assumption of human properties. Therefore, the theological significance of the pre-incarnate "incarnations" of the Son of God needs to be considered. The incarnation is no doubt a divine act of condescension toward man, but it must also be considered as part of the mediator's obedience rendered to the Father according to the eternal covenant of redemption. Jesus described his coming down from heaven in terms of "doing the will of Him who sent Me" (John 6:38), Paul spoke of the incarnation of the Son as an "obedience unto death" (Phil. 2:8), and Hebrews 10:5-7 says:

> Therefore, when He came into the world, He said: "Sacrifice and offering You did not desire, but a body You have prepared for Me. In burnt offerings and sacrifices for sin You had no pleasure. Then I said, 'Behold, I have come—in the volume of the book it is written of Me—to do Your will, O God.'"

Surely the Son's mediatorial work as surety precedes his incarnation, but his actual accomplishment of redemption does not. Oliphint, however, unwittingly provides us with reason to make the further conclusion that the mediator's pre-incarnation "incarnations" were no less part of his active and passive obedience than his actual incarnation. Perhaps this is where his biblical theology not only runs rough shod over systematic theology (all theology becomes Christology), but also woefully fails to account for the progressive nature of redemptive history itself.

Indeed, Oliphint repeatedly states that the actual incarnation is *sui generis,* that is, one of a kind. But saying it is so is not the same as showing that it is so. By making the actual incarnation the consummation, not only of God's redemptive-historical revelation, but of an entire incarnational process since the beginning of the world, Oliphint deprives God of his glory and the incarnation of its wonder and uniqueness.

Perhaps a more fundamental question can be posed, "Why do we need to invent new theological categories in the first place?" The answer to this question seems to lie in at least two assumptions made by the author. First, it appears that in Oliphint's quest to take the relative attributes and anthropomorphisms seriously, he has assumed that language about God must either be univocal or equivocal. This implies that it either has to mean the same thing for God as it does for us, or else it has no meaning at all. Committed to the former, he has sought categories that would affirm both God's aseity and his ability to really and truly grieve, suffer, repent, and so on. Finding his univocal core in Christ, the God-man, he concludes that what may be predicated of Christ incarnate may also be really and truly predicated of God apart from the incarnation. For instance:

> Christ, the Son of God in the flesh, suffered; he died, and he did that as the God-man, the quintessential covenant person. Since that is true, there must be some real and fundamental sense in which God can have or experience passions. (87)

We may wonder how far he would have us press this formula. Hunger, temptation, exhaustion, death, and the like are all predicated of Jesus. Are we to assume that there is "some real and fundamental sense in which God can have or experience" such things? For a Reformed theologian of his caliber, it is perplexing that he has nothing to say about analogical predication, which would both affirm the text's meaning and properly distinguish between the Creator and the creature. This is further evidence of what becomes clear throughout, that he is not engaging in a dialogue from within his own tradition, historically and confessionally understood, but from without.

Second, contrary to Oliphint's stated intent, his proposal assumes a problem-solution approach, wherein God's transcendence is a problem that needs to be overcome before he is able to relate to anything that is not himself. He would insist that this is not the case, for God's so-called covenantal properties do not alter his essential properties. "He limits himself while remaining the infinite God" (188). However, the case remains that, for Oliphint, God cannot relate to his creation, much less create, in his transcendence. It would seem that the incarnation was as necessary to overcome an ontological problem that is no less his than ours, than it was to overcome a sin problem. God neither does nor can relate to us *as God*, but only as he has ontologically condescended *as a creature* by virtue of created properties. Thus, for all of Oliphint's insistence that his proposal preserves God's independence and essential immutability, his particular solution has the unfortunate consequence of making God, *as God*, equally irrelevant.

According to this view, God's transcendence poses a relate-ability problem that must be overcome by taking on created properties. "Once he determines to relate to us, that relation entails that he take on properties that he otherwise would not have had" (188). As we have already observed, in order for God to be Creator he had to ontologically condescend by taking on created covenantal properties. At this point, it should be asked how God, in his transcendence, related himself to the very first covenantal properties that enabled him to create as Creator, for he would need to create covenantal properties to do so. Likewise, he would need to create covenantal properties in order to relate himself to those created properties. There would be an infinite regress of covenantal properties, and thus the *reductio ad absurdum* of Oliphint's proposal.

Why do we need new theological categories in the first place? In *God with Us*, K. Scott Oliphint proposes a novel solution to a theological problem that has been posed by modern liberals and open theists. As is too often the case, the older tradition is dismissed and the presuppositions of the liberals are granted without argument. Early in the book, in an argument against an opposing view, Oliphint states, "One of the questions that should be asked in this regard is why the orthodox tradition did not see the need to posit such things" (77). This is precisely the question Oliphint should have asked the open theists, and we must now ironically ask of Oliphint. Why should it be taken for granted that there is a problem that needs to be solved? Why didn't the orthodox tradition see the need to posit created covenantal properties of God apart from the actual incarnation? Wouldn't a closer examination of the Reformed tradition suggest that much of the contemporary debate assumes a false dilemma between God's transcendence and immanence? Can we even assume that they were asking the same questions? And if not, why not?

Much of the discussion found in this book tends to reveal that the contemporary theological agenda has more or less to do with a desire to affirm the God of Open Theism without a total abandonment of the God of classical theism. And yet, the failure of Oliphint's project reminds us that if we accept their assumption that God's transcendence is a problem that needs to be overcome, then we must also accept with them the conclusion that it is a problem that cannot be overcome. As open theists have declared all along, once their version of relate-ability is more or less affirmed, the God of classical theism cannot merely be revised, he must be abandoned all together.

Process and Providence: The Evolution Question at Princeton, 1845-1929,

Bradley J. Gundlach
(Grand Rapids: Eerdmans, 2013, 374 pp.),
reviewed by James M. Renihan

Old Princeton, that bastion of conservative theology, is famous for its support and defense of Old School Presbyterianism over against the inroads of nineteenth-century Rationalism as well as New School Divinity. Their articulation of a high doctrine of Scripture is especially noteworthy, as it provided an intellectual defense in support of the historic teaching of the church on the nature of special revelation.

The story has often been told, and we have recognized the debt we owe to the Princetonians. But the story has not always been *fully* told, for significant cracks were present in the foundation of the two institutions—The College of New Jersey (Princeton University) and Princeton Theological Seminary. Bradley Gundlach's *Process and Providence: The Evolution Question at Princeton, 1845-1929* details the nature of one of the most significant of those cracks—the willingness of men at both institutions to consider and ultimately make peace with versions of the theory of evolution. Following a chronological path, the author traces the various views held by the leaders of both Seminary and University. The two, though distinct, maintained a close bond through shared faculty and trustees. Among those we meet are James McCosh and Francis Patton, both presidents of the University as well as familiar names from the Seminary. Readers of this *Journal* will be more interested in the story as it relates to the worthies of the Seminary, Charles Hodge and B. B. Warfield in particular, and thus this review will focus there.

The main body of the book opens with a startling citation from Charles Hodge: "History in all its details, even the most minute, is but the evolution of the eternal purposes of God" (1). Hodge was very much a man of his time, and held firmly to a developmental view of the world and all that is in it. Gundlach defines development as "the unfolding of built-in potentials over time and in interaction with the environment" and states that in the eyes of the Princetonians, this "was precisely God's usual way of doing things" (5).

Believing that God's decrees are executed in creation and providence, i.e., by first and second causes, Hodge was able to acknowledge that a divinely directed process of evolution was not outside the purview of the Christian faith. While he named Darwinism as "atheism," he did not reject evolution conceptually. Darwinism, or natural selection by chance, could not be received since it postulated causes and results without divine involvement. Divinely directed development, however, was a very different thing. The processes used in the advance of the world could be explained in terms of sovereign purpose. If God determined that the development of the universe took eons, so be it. If he made Adam from pre-existing animal ancestors (interpreted as "the dust of the earth"), we must accept the possibility. The point is carefully nuanced: "None of the Princeton theologians asserted such a picture of human origins as definite fact; rather they allowed it and at the most held it more or less tentatively" (313). But isn't that the problem? Is a high view of Scripture compatible with any form of human evolutionary theory?

Warfield held similar views. Gundlach cites him: "there is no *necessary* antagonism of Xty to evolution, *provided that* we do not hold to too extreme a form of evolution" (241 spelling and emphasis his). One wonders where the boundary of "extreme" is located. Gundlach demonstrates that Warfield, like Hodge, rejected Darwinism, but shared a similar commitment to development and thus allowed for the possibility of evolution as the divine method.

Princeton Seminary was committed to a philosophical system based on empirical observation and proof. Many years ago, a professor of mine made an interesting statement about Westminster Seminary in Philadelphia. He said that it sat uneasily in the chair of Old Princeton. By this he intended to observe the difference between the presuppositionalist apologetics of the former as over against the essentially rationalist apologetics of the latter. Gundlach helpfully identifies the naïve and optimistic rationalism of the Princeton theologians. Under the influence of Common Sense Realism, they were convinced that honest observers would interpret natural data truthfully. Thus, proper thinking scientists could deduce conclusions from general revelation that would not contradict details of special revelation. Where the Bible is silent, science may fill the gaps. The Princetonians were convinced that theology and progressive science could walk together, so long as the advocates of either did not trespass the boundaries of their disciplines and intrude into the other sphere. This is why Darwinism could be rejected while other theories accepted.

Confessionalism is relevant as well. While Hodge used the *Westminster Confession of Faith* throughout his writings (especially in his *Systematic Theology*), he was not reluctant to interpret it in new ways and invest it with novel meaning. An extended quotation may be useful.

> Hodge believed confessional subscription did not mean unswerving acceptance of every single proposition in the creeds of the church, but acceptance of the system as a whole. That system, however, rested on certain basic doctrines 'no one of which can be omitted without destroying its identity.' Among those foundational doctrines was creation, and Hodge took pains to explain what 'creation' could and could not include. Creation meant 'that the universe and all that it contains is not eternal, is not a necessary product of the life of God, is not an emanation from the divine substance, but owes its existence as to substance and form solely to his will—and in reference to man that he was created in the image of God, in knowledge, righteousness, and holiness and not *in puris naturalibus*, without any moral character.' Noticeably absent from Hodge's detailed list of the sine qua nons of creation was any denial of transmutation. He jealously guarded the distinction of the Creator from his creation, to avoid pantheistic monism. He also contradicted the Roman Catholic view of natural man as all of earth and none of heaven, for in the Reformed view the first great mystery of humankind was the bridging of mind and matter, and even fallen humanity bore the image of God. On both counts he asserted the confessional necessity of metaphysical dualism—and left the evolution question moot. (78)

While the theologians who met in the mid 1640s at Westminster and published what may be the most important confession of faith in the English language never imagined a doctrine of evolution consonant with their views of creation, Hodge was untroubled to allow for its possibility! This is a sweeping denial of strict confessionalism.

The story told is fascinating and disturbing. Fascinating in that it places the Princeton theologians into an enlightening context. For all of the wonderful contributions they made in defense of the Old Faith, they were also profoundly influenced by the intellectual climate in which they lived. Perhaps this is unavoidable, but it is very helpful to recognize such and read the contributions of these men in that light. It is disturbing in that it reveals serious flaws in some theological heroes. Gundlach helps us to understand that there are critical dangers, even for the greatest of men, in loose theological commitments. One may fight with fervor for the doctrine of Scripture while allowing the enemy in the side door of evolution. In the end at Princeton, Scripture (and confessional Reformed theology) lost while evolution triumphed.

Heroes have clay feet, and in this book, Gundlach presents the failings of eminent men. The seeds of Princeton Seminary's demise in 1929 had been present almost from its beginning. The Hodges and Warfield were profoundly influenced by the philosophical milieu in which they lived, and they could not escape. While defending the nature of Scripture as a genuine, inspired and inerrant word from God, they failed to uphold one of its most basic truths (Hebrews 11:3). That which they kept with one hand was given away with the other. Their commitment to a system of doctrine in their Confession without emphasizing its details allowed for a swift demise. This is always the case with loose confessional subscription. Let us take heed. We have benefited mightily from the positive contributions of these men, let us now learn from their mistakes. How much of the climate of the postmodern era affects our theological convictions?

For readers of this *Journal*, Gundlach's volume is timely and very important. It is well worth the investment of time and money, and deserves a thoughtful reading.

The Question of Canon: ***Challenging the Status Quo in the New Testament Debate,***

Michael J. Kruger
(Downers Grove, IL: IVP Academic, 2013, 256pp.),
reviewed by James P. Butler

The Question of Canon (QC) is the latest book by Dr. Michael J. Kruger, President and Professor of New Testament at Reformed Theological Seminary in Charlotte, NC. Like Dr. Kruger's previous book *Canon Revisited* (CR), QC is essential reading for pastors and theological students.

In the Introduction, Kruger sets forth the focus of the book. Unlike CR, which demonstrated the criteria used in specifying which books are considered canonical, QC deals with the very "existence" of canon. According to Kruger, "While the validity of the canon's boundaries is still an area of concern, the attention has shifted to the validity of the canon's very *existence.* The question now is, why is there a New Testament at all?"(17). He introduces two approaches to the question of canon, the extrinsic model and the intrinsic model. The extrinsic model assumes that "the idea of canon was, to some degree, imposed upon the Christian faith" (18). The preferred model, and that which is defended in the remainder of the book, is the "intrinsic model." He explains, "This model suggests that the idea of canon is not something imposed from the outside but develops more organically from within the early Christian religion itself" (21). He ends the Introduction by stating the purpose for the book: it is not to prove the intrinsic model but to show the problems with the five tenets employed by the extrinsic model. The five tenets are: one, there is a sharp distinction between Scripture and canon; two, there was nothing in earliest Christianity that might have led to a canon; three, early Christians were averse to written documents; four, the NT authors were unaware of their own authority; and five, the NT books were first regarded as Scripture at the end of the second century (23-24). The five tenets are each dealt with in subsequent chapters and, in each instance, Kruger shows the problematic nature of the extrinsic model.

The first chapter is concerned with the definition of canon. Kruger says there are three ways to look at the definition. In the first place, the *exclusive* definition describes canon as a fixed, final, and closed list of books. Secondly, the *functional* definition of the canon refers to "the entire process by which the formation of the church's sacred writings took place" (34, quoting Brevard Childs). This means that the term canon can be used as soon as a book is regarded as Scripture (35). Thirdly, the *ontological* definition focuses on what the canon is "in and of itself, namely *the authoritative books that God gave his corporate church*" (40). Kruger highlights the benefits of definitions one and two, but also indicates their shortcomings. Kruger favors the third definition and argues persuasively for its adoption.

In chapter 2, the origins of canon are discussed. He asks the question as to the theological matrix of first-century Christianity and whether or not there was a favorable climate to the growth of a new revelational deposit (48). In the remainder of chapter, 2 he answers in the affirmative. Firstly, the eschatological nature of early Christianity argues for the growth of such a deposit. First-century Christians viewed the OT as incomplete; the promises were to find fulfilment and they did so in the coming of the Lord Jesus. Secondly, the concept of covenant in early Christianity argues for the growth of such a deposit. The people of God have always been a people of the book. The Old Covenant was accompanied by written texts; so was the New Covenant. Kruger highlights some of the similarities between the written texts of the Old and New Covenants; a very helpful section for those committed to covenant theology. Thirdly, the role of the apostles in early Christianity argues for the growth of such a deposit. The apostles were invested with the authority of Christ himself, and as a result, they were his "authorized agents to deliver and transmit the new message of redemption" (77).

In chapter 3, the writing of canon is discussed. He quotes several scholars who argue that early Christians were so inclined to an "oral" form of religion, that they would have been hesitant to "place value on written documents" (79). Kruger deals with the three arguments proffered by such proponents. First, the argument from the socio-historical background: early Christianity was an oral culture. He shows that orality and textuality are not mutually exclusive. He then proves that early Christianity was in fact textual in nature. Secondly, the argument from testimony: early Christians expressly stated their aversion to writing. Kruger discusses Papias and Paul and shows that this second objection does not stand muster. Thirdly, the argument from eschatology: early Christians expected the imminent return of Christ. Kruger shows that this objection is also without foundation: even if the early Christians expected an imminent return, it does not necessarily inhibit literary production.

In chapter 4, the authors of canon are discussed. Those who challenge the question of canon assert that the apostles did not have an awareness of their role in the revelational process. Kruger states the thesis of chapter 4 as follows:

> the New Testament authors, generally speaking, demonstrate awareness that their writings passed down authentic apostolic tradition and therefore bore supreme authority in the life of the church. (121)

He then briefly discusses key passages in the Pauline letters, the Gospels, and other New Testament writings. He demonstrates, beyond a shadow of a doubt, that the NT authors had a conscious awareness of their role in the revelational process. He ends the chapter by stating:

> Thus, the existence of a new covenantal deposit of books was not due simply to Marcion's heresies or to later church politics [theories propounded in the extrinsic model], but to the intentional activities of the New Testament writers themselves. (154)

In chapter 5, the date of the canon is addressed. The proponents of the extrinsic model point specifically to statements made by Irenaeus. Kruger explains:

> The reason for this focus on the end of the second century is not hard to find. It is at this point that the major figure Irenaeus, bishop of Lyons, offers some of the clearest and most comprehensive statements on the canon to date. (156-57)

Kruger discusses the particular statements of Irenaeus and then looks at other key evidence, contemporaries of Irenaeus. Here, Kruger appeals to the Muratorian fragment, Theophilus of Antioch, and Clement of Alexandria. Kruger states:

> Thus, we see a clear pattern emerging. At the end of the second century, it appears that Irenaeus is not alone. According to the Muratorian fragment, Theophilus of Antioch and Clement of Alexandria (not to mention Tatian)—influential and geographically diverse sources at the end of the second century—there was a core collection of scriptural books in place that the church fathers themselves did not view as newly established. (169)

He then cites from Justin Martyr, the apostolic fathers, and the NT documents themselves to show that predecessors to Irenaeus recognized canonical Scriptures, early in the second century and even in the middle to late first century. In the conclusion to chapter 5, Kruger reminds the reader:

> One should also not forget that the evidence above is not just from a single church father, but from a variety of sources spread over a number of different regions. While any individual piece of evidence might be contested or questioned, it is the extent of the evidence that proves to be the compelling factor. (203)

Kruger ends with a helpful conclusion that summarizes the preceding chapters very well. He rehearses the five tenets that were given in the introduction and discussed in chapters 1-5. In brief compass he gives a helpful summary of why these tenets of the extrinsic model are problematic.

The church is indebted to Dr. Kruger. Pastors especially should avail themselves of both QC and CR (in that order in my opinion) as the question of canon "is at the very center of how biblical authority is established" (CR, 16). The church will continue to be challenged concerning their sacred writings and it is certainly the responsibility of those pastors who serve on the front lines to be able to give a defense to whoever asks, whether questions come from the atheist professor at the local university, or the eight year old in Sunday School.

The Theology of the Westminster Standards: Historical Context and Theological Insights,
John V. Fesko
(Wheaton: Crossway, 2014, 441 pp.),
and
Confessing the Faith: A Reader's Guide to the Westminster Confession of Faith,
Chad Van Dixhoorn
(Edinburgh: The Banner of Truth Trust, 2014, 484 pp.),
reviewed by James M. Renihan

In the past year, these two important and useful works on the documents of the Westminster Assembly have appeared. Taking different approaches to the material, they complement each other well. Each seeks to examine the theology produced by the Assembly, placing it into its proper historical context and demonstrating the internal coherence of the doctrine contained therein.

The title of John Fesko's book must be noted—it is an examination of theology in the Westminster *Standards*—i.e., not simply the teaching of the famous Confession of Faith, but also the other documents produced by the Assembly, most notably the Larger and Shorter Catechisms. For this reason, the book approaches theology topically, though the order of chapters in the Confession does serve as the basis for its forward movement. He devotes chapters to Scripture, God and the decree, covenant and creation, Christology, justification, sanctification, the Law of God and the Christian life, the church, worship, and eschatology. There is a wealth of useful material in each of these chapters.

Chad Van Dixhoorn's work is more specifically focused on the Confession, following the order of the chapters and commenting on each paragraph throughout. But it is a 'Reader's Guide.' It is not an exhaustive examination of every word or even doctrine taught in the Confession, but rather a helpful tool for the general reader to understand more fully the emphases of each chapter. In his preface, the author refreshingly says, "the church needs to experiment with theological maximalism in place of its current minimalism" (xii). Perhaps these volumes will contribute to that recovery of a full system of theological belief. We need confessions—full, carefully constructed, and detailed—rather than abbreviated doctrinal statements. These texts help us to understand the wonderful and God-honoring purpose of well-developed and thorough systems of theology.

Drs. Fesko and Van Dixhoorn are acknowledged experts on the seventeenth-century context of the Westminster Assembly, and this expertise shines through both volumes. Each of the authors recognize that the only proper method of interpreting an old document is to read it in its context, letting contemporary thought illumine the nature of what it meant and what it means. They have successfully avoided the postmodern trap of reader response interpretation—the 'what it means to me' syndrome. Historical documents have a fixed context, and understanding that context is essential to proper interpretation. Readers may disagree with that context and its conclusions, but they must do so honestly, recognizing that they are departing from the established sense of the original authors. These books help advance a proper reading of the texts.

John Fesko's book carefully demonstrates the *catholic* nature of Reformed theology in its Westminster forms. He says:

> Unlike our own day, when Reformed theologians are content to labor for their entire ministries in theologically sectarian-like settings where orthodoxy is measured by a very narrow set of criteria, the Westminster divines had a different index by which they measured orthodoxy. The divines considered themselves *reformed* Catholics and therefore did not want to isolate themselves from the rest of the church, but saw their broader engagement with other periods of history and other theological traditions as evidence of their catholicity. (29)

What a refreshing notion! Too many today reject the riches of the history of the church, or use *ad hominem* arguments to support a narrow modern evangelical perspective on theology. As the heirs of great classical systems, we only harm ourselves and those we teach when we advocate novelties promoted by contemporaries. Our Particular Baptist fathers would have recognized this methodology. It is not surprising when reading Nehemiah Coxe or Benjamin Keach to find citations from fathers like Augustine and Chrysostom, medievals such as Aquinas or Grosseteste, and continental Roman Catholics like Vatablus (†1547) or Mercerus (†1570).

Another virtue of these books is their honesty in demonstrating that theology and practice in the Puritan era sometimes significantly differed from modern evangelicalism. In his exposition of Chapter 14, *Of Saving Faith,* Van Dixhoorn demonstrates that the Reformed faith unashamedly promotes preaching as the primary and ordinary means God uses to save and sanctify sinners. The text of the Confession says:

> The grace of faith, whereby the elect are enabled to believe to the saving of their souls, is the work of the Spirit of Christ in their hearts, and is ordinarily wrought by the ministry of the Word, by which also, and by the administration of the sacraments, and prayer, it is increased and strengthened.

In the elucidation of this doctrine, Van Dixhoorn cites the Westminster divine Anthony Burgess, who states, "The Ministry is the only ordinary way that God hath appointed, either for the beginnings or increase of grace" and then Jeremiah Burroughs who wrote "because God hath appointed this to be his ordinance, therefore in obedience to him [they] wil[l] attend upon this means rather than upon other means" (186-87). It's not about methods and programs that God commands—it's the simple method of preaching by appointed men. This is the teaching of the Westminster Confession, as well as that of the Second London Confession. Too often good men have been influenced by the culture of evangelicalism and fail to recognize that their methods depart from the Reformed faith. They fail to be truly confessional at those points. Perhaps these books will help to recover them to consistency.

While the Westminster Confession does differ from our own Second London Confession in some significant ways, these two books will be immensely helpful for every Reformed Baptist. With the growing body of literature available to us, we really must understand our Confession as it was written and intended. It is *not* an evangelical document (as that term is understood today), it is a Reformed document and functions precisely in this way. To hold it faithfully, we must seek to understand it completely and to live it out carefully. May God give us his help.

Thomas Aquinas's* Summa Theologiae*: A Guide and Commentary,
Brian Davies
(New York: Oxford University Press, 2014, xvi + 454pp.),
reviewed by James E. Dolezal

Since the publication of *The Thought of Thomas Aquinas* (Clarendon, 1992) Brian Davies has carved out a niche for himself as something of a specialist in writing non-specialist introductions to Thomas Aquinas. This volume is longer and more narrowly focused than his previous introductions as he seeks to guide readers step by step through the text of Thomas' *Summa Theologiae*. It bears some similarity to his 1992 volume insofar as that volume also tends to follow the order of the greater *Summa*, yet this is a truer guide to the text and development of the *Summa* itself. It differs from other studies on the *Summa* in that it is neither a full-scale critical analysis nor merely a paraphrase of Thomas's landmark work. Rather, as Davies states, "I try to explain what Thomas argues in the *Summa Theologiae* while providing more than a mere paraphrase of it. . . . I also try to locate the *Summa* historically and to note the extent to which Thomas was influenced by people writing before and by traditions that he inherited, and I write while hoping to prod readers into thinking about it critically" (xiii).

Protestants in particular tend to be either entirely ignorant of Thomas' teaching or they presume to know something of what he believed based on hearsay; either way they are generally underexposed to the actual writings and flow of thought of the famous Dominican friar. Davies' volume is a wonderful tool for reversing this ignorance and for guiding uninitiated readers through one of the most remarkable works in the history of Christian theology. A Dominican priest himself, Davies does not try to adjust Thomas' teaching to suit modern sensibilities (be they conservative Protestant, liberal, progressive Roman Catholic, or secularist) or downplay his medieval Catholicism in any way. Overall, Davies provides a fairly dispassionate read of the *Summa* that will serve as a reliable manual to readers who simply want to know what Thomas teaches through the many passages of his *magnum opus*. This volume can be read straight through, though it can also be used as a handbook.

The twenty-three chapters are extensively subdivided to facilitate easy access to Davies's discussion on each section of the *Summa*. Thomas' complete text is not reproduced and Davies does not offer commentary on every single question. He does a good job, though, of explaining why he omits certain material, usually due either to its similarity to other questions Davies has already discussed or to its uniquely myopic focus being too obscure for discussion in a single-volume overview. Readers seeking extended technical explanations will have to look elsewhere.

An outstanding strength of Davies' overview method is that it gives readers a sense of the movement of the *Summa* as a whole. Why does Thomas' treatment progress as it does? Davies is alert to such questions. Also, given the density of Thomas' text and subtly of his arguments Davies does an admirable job making the arguments accessible by offering numerous real world illustrations and by carefully explaining at times what Thomas does *not* mean. The author is keenly aware of those areas of Thomas' thought that will cause the most confusion to modern readers and is careful to explain terms and intended meanings. Another virtue of the work is Davies' refutation of some of the more influential recent critics of Thomas (e.g., Anthony Kenny). Davies does not critique such scholars for disagreeing with Thomas' doctrine (the book is not a defense of Thomism) but for misreading his text. These correctives are useful, and Davies is sparing in polemic so as not to overwhelm his aim of producing a positive exposition of Thomas' text.

So what of the book's content? Inasmuch as it covers a vast theological terrain, I shall focus on a couple representative portions that may be of particular interest to Reformed readers.

Not surprisingly, Davies offers a somewhat extended discussion of Thomas' famous "Five Ways" for demonstrating God's existence (34-50). Especially helpful is his explanation of what Thomas is and is not seeking to accomplish in these arguments. His arguments are often criticized for not establishing that God has *all* the attributes Christians ascribe to him. The charge is that Thomas' "proofs" give us bare theism. Davies counters that Thomas was not trying to make the totality of God's existence clear in the Five Ways, but more modestly that he was simply attempting to get the ball rolling in the discussion of God's being. He was seeking to show that natural knowledge of God is possible. In reality, Thomas' arguments for God's existence in the *Summa* extend all the way through his discussion of God's attributes and triunity (to Ia.45).

As for God as the first cause of being, which is the basic contention running through the Five Ways, Davies clarifies that Thomas' argument is not that God is the first in a *per accidens* series who simply gets the series of being started (e.g., as the first link on a great chain of being), but that he is the first cause of the series of being *per se* (e.g., as the one who gives existence to the entire chain of being all along the line and is not himself one of the things in the series) (35). God is not the first cause or "mover" chronologically, but the first inasmuch as he is the most fundamental source and explanation of contingent being wherever and whenever it is found. This interpretation effectually refutes the old accusation that Thomas' Five Ways teach God is the first link on the great chain of being with creatures and thus stands univocally with them in the same order of being. This would only be true if Thomas were speaking of a *per accidens* series, but not if he were referring to a *per se* one as Davies argues. It seems to me that this is probably why our Reformed forebears did not criticize Thomas' Five Ways for falling into the error of ontological univocism and were comfortable reproducing many of his same arguments.

Another area that will be of particular interest to Reformed readers is Davies' discussion of Thomas on grace, justification, and merit (223-29). It is not uncommon that contemporary Protestant critics of Roman Catholic teaching read back into medieval Catholics the doctrines of Tridentine Catholicism and the Semipelagianism of sixteenth-century Jesuits. But this approach can be rather anachronistic and distortive of the actual teachings of the medieval theologians.

For Thomas grace is nothing but a human participation in the divine nature (following 2 Pet. 1:3-4). Davies explains that Thomas's teaching does not diminish the absolute distinction between God and creatures, but rather concludes that such a radical distinction entails that in granting grace to creatures "God lifts people to a state that *only* God can bring them to, a state that reflects what only God is or has by *nature*" (223). Because grace is a creaturely participation in God it follows that God alone can grant it.[1] Moreover, this is not a state into which man may move himself by his natural powers: "[O]ur becoming more like God than we can by our own efforts is what Thomas takes to be the work of grace" (224). People cannot even prepare themselves for grace without the assistance of grace (225). This is rather plainly at odds with later Jesuit teaching that men prepare themselves to receive grace by doing what is in them by nature. Also, while Thomas's emphasis upon grace as an exclusively divine work is quite agreeable to Reformed conviction, his belief that man cannot naturally or deductively, but only inductively or by private revelation, know he is graced is rather more perplexing (226).

Thomas' teaching on justification is less amenable to Reformed and Lutheran conviction. He takes justifying grace to be not only a matter of God forgiving our sins, but also a matter of us acting in accordance with God's will. Inasmuch as forgiveness is inseparable from repentance and repentance is an ongoing process, so Thomas believes justification is an ongoing process. Davies is clear that Aquinas believes God's justification of humans corresponds to the

---

1 For Thomas and most other medieval theologians "participation" signifies imitation and does not mean that humans meld into God ontologically.

actual progress in holiness attained by those humans (227). In other words, Thomas has no place for Luther's teaching that the Christian is made just simply by God's declaration or that the Christian can be at the same time just and sinner (*simul justus et peccator*). The Christian is only just to the extent that he has been actually transformed by God's grace. Again, as this transformation is a process, so is justification.

Obviously, Thomas lacks the doctrine of the imputation of alien righteousness which is so fundamental to Lutheran and Reformed belief about justification. On the other hand, he does not seem to accept the Semi-pelagian notion (espoused by so many Jesuits and modern Roman Catholics) that man is naturally able to attain justifying grace. All progress in grace is caused by God so that man does not earn justification according to the exercise of his natural human capacities. Thomas seems to avoid the charge of Semi-pelagianism, though, from the Reformed perspective, he still wrongly identifies the righteousness upon which God bases his justifying verdict.

Finally, Davies argues that Thomas adjusts his notion of merit to suit his understanding of God and grace. Thomas holds that "while certain people might rightly claim a reward from others for what they have done, nobody can claim a reward from God absolutely speaking" (229). He bases this on the absolute inequality between God and humans. If God regards any human works to be meritorious it can only be on account of his having freely chosen to regard them as such. God graciously ordains to give rewards to humans for their work and action. Davies summarizes Thomas' teaching: "We have no claim in justice to anything from God, yet God has arranged that we, as freely choosing creatures, can merit from God in terms of God's will and grace" (229). Meritorious reward, then, depends entirely on God's grace and not on human achievements. Thomas thinks we can merit eternal life through acts of charity but the grace in us that produces acts of charity is not itself something he thinks we can merit. Growth in good works "depends only on the divine motion, which is the principle and source of all merit" (229, citing *Summa Theologiae* IaIIae.114.9). In sum, the grace in us that produces meritorious works is not itself a reward for our good works. Rather it is God working in us for our good. As with the doctrine of justification, Thomas' teaching on merit proscribes the Semi-pelagian notion that man's good works strictly merit God's grace in his life. Yet it still assumes that God does not give rewards, such as eternal life, to those who have not been made actually holy by the process of gracious transformation. From the Reformed perspective Thomas lacks the doctrine of imputation and conceives justification and merit strictly along the lines of infused and transformative grace.

These few examples are only a very small sampling of the wide ranging discussion found in Davies' volume. The value of his work is in placing the thought of Thomas within its original context. It also enables Protestant readers to form a more objective understanding of what Thomas actually taught. Some of his teaching is in fundamental agreement with Reformed conviction and is even formative of later Reformed orthodox thought (e.g., on the doctrine of God), while other aspects of it are quite different from the Reformed view (e.g., on the sacraments or aspects of justification). Either way we can be thankful that Davies has produced such an unprejudiced and reliable guide to this most mature development of Thomas Aquinas' theology. This is arguably the finest single-volume guide to the *Summa Theologiae* available and is deserving of a place on the bookshelves of scholars and pastors alike.

Thomas Grantham: God's Messenger from Lincolnshire,
John Inscore Essick
(Macon, GA: Mercer University Press, 2013, 246 pp.),
reviewed by James M. Renihan

English Baptist historiography has followed a meandering course. Early in the twentieth century, greater interest was shown in General Baptists, since they were the first to appear in the seventeenth century. Later, recognizing that the Particular Baptists had actually made larger contributions to the movement as a whole, the focus of attention tended to shift to studies about them. Recently, more material about General Baptists has begun to appear. This is a positive development. John Inscore Essick's biography of Thomas Grantham is a welcome addition to this body of literature.

Thomas Grantham (1633/34-1692) may have been the most important and influential leader among the General Baptists in the second half of the seventeenth century. This is certainly true of Lincolnshire and the surrounding counties, but may be just as true nationally. During a difficult period of persecution and opposition, he provided leadership to a struggling movement, planting churches and encouraging congregations to press on.

The book examines several aspects of Grantham's life and career. Beginning with a detailed biographical chapter, it explores his published works, his major ecclesiological contributions, his debates with non-Baptists, and his political views. Each chapter locates Grantham in his own context and helpfully describes both the influences upon him as well as his contributions. Two areas deserve notice—his promotion of the office of 'messenger' in the churches, and his theological writings.

A unique ecclesiological development among the General Baptists was the adoption of the office of 'messenger.' Added to elder or pastor and deacon, 'messengers' were a formal third office functioning among the churches at large. Grantham's published writings described and defended the office from Scripture, arguing that while Apostles (note the upper case 'A') were no longer present on earth, it was God's will that apostles (lower case 'a') should continue to operate in the churches. These were 'messengers' and they served a limited apostolic role as church planters but also as superintendents over the churches in particular geographic areas. Timothy and Titus were something of models for the office and texts such as Titus 1:5 helped define its duties. For all intents and purposes, this was a Baptist version of the office of bishop, and its support was similar to what one might find among contemporary Episcopalian writers. Grantham was its greatest advocate, and served in that role himself. While Particular Baptists also employed the term messenger, they invested it with a very different meaning. For them, a messenger was simply a representative of a local congregation. This might have been at an association meeting, or it might have been to carry communiqués from one church to another. The messenger had a limited function, serving the specific purpose appointed by the congregation, carrying no authority beyond his representative responsibility. General Baptist ecclesiology was much more connectional than that of the Particulars, and this office of messenger helps to account for that strong denominationalism. Of course, the presence of this view demonstrates the false nature of the claim that Baptists have always promoted a strong doctrine of the autonomy of the local church. Such claims must be carefully nuanced.

Demographically, General Baptists and Particular Baptists tended to occupy different areas of England. The Particulars flourished in areas where Puritan Congregational churches also prospered, and the Generals tended to be located in areas with a stronger Episcopalian presence. One wonders if the related ecclesiologies might not reflect these differences. Particular Baptist practice was essentially the same as the Puritan Congregationalists with whom they more closely identified; General Baptist practiced resembled, *in some sense*, that of the Church of England.

Grantham's systematic theology is found in his large corpus of writings, but is principally located in his magnum opus, *Christianismus Primitivus* (1678). While William Brackney's claim (in the foreword) that Grantham was 'the first systematic theologian among the Baptists' (unnumbered page ii) is an overstatement,[1] he did produce a major work in presentation of General Baptist theology. Essick judiciously weaves the major themes of *Christianismus Primitivus* into his story, demonstrating Grantham's reasoning ability. It is clearly a *General Baptist* theology, reflecting all of the expected emphases of that group. The present volume does not explore the significant differences between the two Baptist groups (in fact, it seems that Grantham had very little contact with

[1] Among the General Baptists, William Jeffrey preceded Grantham by nearly 20 years with his *The Whole Faith of Man*.

Particular Baptists). This might have been a useful addition to the argument of the book. Grantham is known, for example, to have advocated the Arminian view that men may be saved by living up to the light they receive apart from explicit faith in Christ.[2] This is directly contrary to the views of the Particular Baptists. An exposition of the profound contrast in this (and perhaps other) views would have been appreciated.

John Inscore Essick's exposition of the life and work of Thomas Grantham is an important contribution to our knowledge of early English Baptists. It is a valuable and helpful exposition of a significant but little known figure from General Baptist history.

---

[2] For example, Grantham wrote in *Christianismus Primitivus*, "though all nations had not at all times the Law and the Prophets to read, and to inform them in the knowledge of Christ, yet it is to admiration what discoveries were made concerning Him . . . ," 56. For more detail, see my article "That Strong Hold of Their Common Faith" in *Journal of the Institute of Reformed Baptist Studies* (2014): 79-81.